*L*etters *H*ome

Letters Home

How Writing Can Change Your Life

TERRY VANCE, PH.D.

PANTHEON BOOKS

NEW YORK

Grateful acknowledgment is made to the following for permission to reprint previously published material: *Bantam Books*: Excerpt from "Hope as an Obstacle" from *Peace Is Every Step* by Thich Nhat Hanh (Bantam Books, 1991). Reprinted by permission of Bantam Books, a division of Random House, Inc. • *Doubleday*: Excerpts from *Healing and the Mind* by Bill Moyers. Copyright © 1993 by Public Affairs Television and David Grubin Productions Inc. Reprinted by permission of Doubleday, a division of Random House, Inc. • *James Pennebaker*: Excerpt from "Disclosure of Trauma and Immune Function Health Implications for Psychotherapy" by James Pennebaker, J. K. Kiecolt-Glaser, and R. Glaser (*Journal of Consulting and Clinical Psychology* 56, 1988). Reprinted by permission of James Pennebaker • *Science News*: Excerpt from "Sudden Recall: Adult Memories of Child Abuse Spark a Heated Debate" by Bruce Bower (*Science News*, September 18, 1993). Copyright © 1993 by Science Service. Reprinted by permission of *Science News*, the weekly newsmagazine of science.

Library of Congress Cataloging-in-Publication Data

Vance, Terry.
Letters home : how writing can change your life / Terry Vance.
p. cm.
ISBN 0-375-70902-9
1. Letter writing—Therapeutic use. 2. Psychotherapy. I. Title.
RC489.W75V36 1998 616.89'165—dc21 98-10380 CIP

Random House Web Address: *www.randomhouse.com*

Book design by Mia Risberg

Printed in the United States of America
First Paperback Edition
9 8 7 6 5 4 3 2 1

For my mother and father, Ione and Arthur Goldman,
For my husband, Bob,
my sons, Aaron and Brandon,
and my sister, Laurel

Freedom is what you do with what's been done to you.

—JEAN-PAUL SARTRE

CONTENTS

ACKNOWLEDGMENTS

I want to thank my courageous clients: those whose letters are included in this book, and those whose letters are not included either because of space constraints or because doing so might have interfered with their ongoing therapy. Thanks also to those clients who critiqued and supported the letter writers in their therapy groups. Letter therapy has been a joint discovery and collaboration with my clients from the beginning.

I especially want to thank the woman referred to as Dr. B. Her letters to her parents made me realize that writing confrontational letters could profoundly change a person's life. A few years ago, Dr. B. was diagnosed with cancer. Because she had terminated therapy and moved to another state, she began writing letters to me as a way to deal with her feelings about having cancer. Five months before her death, I told her that I was writing *Letters Home,* inspired in part by her early letters. I asked whether she would let me include these letters. We both knew she would not be alive when the book was completed. She was pleased that her letters might help others in similar circumstances.

Thanks to my colleagues and supervisees, who helped me refine letter writing as a therapy method and encouraged me to write this book: my cotherapists Bob Vaillancourt (who gave me the idea for the title and contributed to the last chapter), Vivian Foushee, and Charles Kronberg, and my supervisees Kathy Wayland, Barbara Keyworth, Kathy Putnam, Lea Decker, Jean Livermore Byassee, Chuck Sanislow, and Genie Bailey. Nan Kwock, our do-everything office manager, helped keep me sane during the writing of this book and offered steady encouragement.

Invaluable suggestions along the way came from Gerald Nelson, Cathy Davidson, Jonathan Galassi, Alan Thomas, and especially Alice Kaplan. Alice's enthusiastic support inspired editors to read *Letters Home*. Claudine O'Hearn, my editor at Pantheon, has been both fun to work with and endowed with a remarkable talent for organization, which significantly improved the book's structure.

Robert Carson, chair of my dissertation committee at Duke, is a brilliant mentor and teacher. His delightful humor, wisdom, and perspective have influenced the way I think about the therapeutic process and the nature of change.

The longer I practice psychotherapy, the more I appreciate my parents' love, support, warmth, humor, and wisdom. My mother's insight and perceptiveness about people and their motivations inspired me to become a psychologist. She enthusiastically and thoughtfully critiqued three successive drafts of *Letters Home*. I wish my father were alive to give his reading; it would have been funny and incisive.

My sister, novelist Laurel Goldman, kept me going when I discovered that this project was harder than I thought it would be.

Her merciless editing and keen critiques were invaluable in shaping *Letters Home*. I could not have written it without her.

My sons had doubts, based on historical reality, that I would write this book. Aaron made bets with me about deadlines (I never won), but his teasing expectations spurred me on to keep at it. He did a literature search after I had written the first draft so that I would be educated about experimental research. He ferreted out pockets of fuzzy writing and thinking. Brandon suggested I include a discussion of how the letter writers revised and improved their letters. He convinced me I needed to let the reader know outcomes.

My husband, Bob, has been solidly there for me for over thirty years, and he has profoundly influenced and changed me. His certainty that I would finish this book, his brilliant critiques of each successive draft, and his patient guidance through computer territory in spite of my bad attitude inspired and sustained me. I knew that if he thought this book was good, it was.

The letters included in this book appear as originally written except that identifying names or descriptions are changed and, sometimes, material has been omitted to protect the privacy of the writers and their families or to avoid repetition. Each letter is a real letter written by a real person; there are no composite letters. I regret that there was not room to include all the excellent and remarkable letters my clients have written over the years.

PREFACE

Don't be ashamed to say
what you are not ashamed to think.
— MONTAIGNE

Most of the clients my cotherapists and I see are bright, mo-tivated, good people who have been successful in impor-tant ways. Some have grown up in poverty and were the first in their family to go to college. Others were raised in families of privilege. In spite of their accomplishments, most of them have trouble being honest and open about what they feel and think. They expend enormous energy hiding, appeasing, and living up to others' expectations. This leaves them angry, resentful, unfulfilled, and afraid. They are still trying to win their parents' love and ap-proval, even if they do not like their parents and even if their par-ents are dead. Many of these men and women have in some way been mistreated or neglected by trusted parents who were sup-posed to be nurturing caretakers. Most have moved away from home but have unwittingly trained others to take the same abu-sive or neglectful stance toward them that their parents did. They do this so that they can have the same bad, but reassuringly familiar, feelings, and outcomes. Some of them have a hard time knowing what they feel. In the most extreme circumstances, if the feelings are extraordinarily painful, they dissociate (separate themselves) from their feelings and thoughts so that they will not have to experience the pain.

These clients often grew up with the belief, prevalent in our culture and reinforced in their families, that mistakes are irrevocable. When this view of mistakes is combined with a taboo on expressing angry or hurt feelings and critical thoughts, children become secretive adults who mask their feelings by hiding them or pretending to have feelings they do not have. But masks harm, even deaden, the person underneath.

Getting healthy requires becoming visible by taking off the masks and exposing the secrets—finding out who you are by discovering what you feel and think. To do this you cannot view mistakes as indelible. You cannot see being right as more important than being willing to make successive approximations to the truth. A common excuse for not revealing angry or critical feelings is "I might not be right about what happened." True. You may be wrong. But how are you going to find out if you never say what you are angry about? When no one talks about his critical, angry, or hurt feelings, there is no chance to clear up the communication. Eventually, the unexpressed negative feelings can corrode what positive feelings there are. The first step in confirming or trashing a hypothesis is to bring it out of the dark closet of your private thoughts and into the open air. Tell your version. Tell it to the person you are in conflict with. There is no way to correct, confirm, or add to your view unless you express it. To wait until you know you are right or until you can perfectly express it is to wait forever.

Nineteen years ago, I began assigning letter writing to clients who were afraid to express their feelings to important people in their lives, most often their parents. Their inability to express feelings left these clients in conflict, desperate to move on with their lives but tied up in the past. Initially, I thought of letter writing as a crutch, preparatory to "real" communication, but over the years I discovered that this form of letter writing enables people to fully express what they think and feel. The writers can free themselves from crippling conflicts and impasse even when there is no "real" (face-to-face) communication. Letter writing has proved an effective, goal-oriented way to work out these conflicts. Because the letters are documents that can be reread, progress is easily measured and concretely visualized.

The letter-writing system is designed to express any honest feeling, not just negative or critical feelings. Whether the letters deal with abuse or with less dramatic or damaging behavior, the principles of honest letter writing endure. In some families all feelings are taboo—even joyous feelings are considered excessive or inappropriate, so that showing positive emotions or "appreciations" that have been left unsaid is often as difficult as expressing criticisms. Although many of the letters reprinted here deal with anger and conflict, the point of writing them is to get through the conflict to understanding. I call this honest letter writing, "confrontational" letter writing, in order to distinguish it from ordinary letter writing. But "confrontation" often has a defiant or hostile connotation. There is no word in the English language that gets at what I want: an up-front confrontation with reality that has neither negative nor positive implications. Throughout the text I use the terms "confrontational," "up-front," and "straightforward" interchangeably to convey the neutral meaning I intend. The goal of letter therapy, whatever its focus, is to communicate from the heart in a way that opens up new possibilities for intimacy and growth.

I would have liked to include responses to the letters in the book. They include open and loving attempts to deal with the letter, "guilt trips," scantily disguised death threats, and a flowery card with an inane preprinted message. For obvious ethical and legal reasons, I cannot include them. Nevertheless, the reader can get a good idea of the responses because I either summarize the responses or include a series of letters, which give a sense of the responses elicited, since they refer directly to the response letters.

The fact that, with one exception, the letters in this book were written by people who are or were in therapy is not what matters. These letters simply illustrate the principles of confrontational letter writing, which anyone can use. The letters reprinted here should be useful not just to other therapists and clients but to many who do not need therapy, do not want it, or cannot afford it. Letter writing of this sort is for anyone who wants to work out a conflict and can express his or her feelings in writing.

I hope that the letters will strike a chord that will make it easier for the readers of *Letters Home* to articulate their experiences and that the principles of confrontational letter writing will help future letter writers and responders. Finally, I hope that the stories contained in these letters will shed light on the nature of personal relationships and inspire readers to make the changes they want to make.

PART I

Letters for a Change

*She's leaving home
after living alone for so many years.*

—THE BEATLES

I

Benefiting from the Ease and Safety that Writing Allows

In a more perfect world, we might have the opportunity to be in family therapy or in a similar situation where we are encouraged to confront the truth and are supported for being authentic with the people who are most important to us. But even when parents or significant others are alive and available, it is unusual for everyone in a family to be able and willing to come together for this purpose. In rare cases, the parents can travel and take the time to come to therapy and are not afraid to talk openly, but the resources required in terms of money and therapy time make such a practice prohibitive for most people. Individual or even group therapy is a luxury many people cannot afford or would never consider.

Most people, though, can put their feelings on paper, write a letter to parents, have a friend or spouse or sibling read the letter and give feedback, or put the letter away and reread it later with the enhanced perspective a little distance can give. Although writing letters to deal with important emotional issues is easier with the insight and support that therapy gives, writing an up-front letter does not usually necessitate being in psychotherapy. In cases of abuse, however, the guidance of a qualified therapist is essential. Letter writing (especially when the letter is sent) can help accomplish what family therapy or couples therapy often does. It can bring the significant people together and help the writer separate his contribution to the problem from his parents' or spouse's in a way that is documented and can be gone over and over in different states of mind.

Writing letters is an ordinary activity; it is a tool we all know how to use. When I assign a letter as a part of therapy, it usually does not feel artificial or awkward for the client. The writer can write a letter and wait to show it until he is comfortable with it. Feedback on the feelings that emerge in the letters and the feelings that remain hidden can provide the material and push for the next draft. It feels good and reduces stress to get clear on feelings with specific examples of events and situations that have been suppressed or repressed.[1] Getting out feelings, memories, and thoughts often allows other previously unconscious feelings, memories, and thoughts to emerge. It starts the juices flowing.

Many people who can write a very frank letter are paralyzed by the thought of an in-person confrontation with the most impor-tant figures in their lives. For these people, direct expression of feelings may have been punished violently or less blatantly with constant criticism or humiliation. Feelings may have been con-sistently ignored or discounted. Often there has been no model-ing of how to express a feeling appropriately. Such early patterns make any emotions, especially negative or critical ones, difficult to acknowledge, much less to express to another person.

People who do not feel safe making mistakes or expressing

their feelings in person are usually willing to write a letter that does not have to be sent or even shown to anyone. It can be full of mistakes. It can be revised. If I am afraid to test my perceptions and feelings about what happened because I am afraid of being wrong or of getting mistreated or attacked for expressing feelings that are taboo in my family, I might be willing to see what happens when I express them in writing.

We may hope that if only we express them the "right way," our feelings will be recognized as valid, understood, and appreciated. Or we may fear that if we express ourselves honestly we will be disinherited, hated, or irrevocably harmed or that telling our feelings will destroy a parent—that he or she will have a heart attack or go crazy. These fears and hopes prevent us from letting go of a bondage that can keep us mired in the past.[2] Too much is riding on the communication when the consequences are seen as so momentous. Writing letters that do not have to be sent can create a sense of safety for the writer in the same way that a child can create a sense of safety by using make-believe to pretest, to try out something before it counts for real.[3] Pretending is like a partial reality test that does not require leaving the safety of nonreality.[4] Throughout the history of psychotherapy, many theorists and practitioners have used forms of pretending to help clients change.[5] Increasingly sophisticated studies demonstrate that pretending, "acting" an action, merely acting happy or sad, for instance, can create immediate changes at even the cellular and chemical level.

Margaret Kemeny, a psychologist trained in immunology and psychoneuroimmunology at the University of California, Los Angeles, found that when actors acted either happy or sad, this affected the actors' immune systems, increasing the number of natural killer cells in their bloodstreams. Her conclusion is that expressing any feeling, positive or negative, is healthy. Such research demonstrates that expressed behavior can change a person even if the behavior is at a practice or pretend level.[6]

In addition, expressing feelings and thoughts in a letter has the potential to change the letter writer (even if the letter is never sent) by increasing the writer's recognition that she can behave differently. Writing a draft of a letter creates a temporary responsibility shift similar in its results to the exploratory quality in children's pretending. Exploration works best when trials are felt to be just that; they do not count for keeps. This is why an assignment to write a letter will often get carried out only when the writer is reminded that she does not have to send it even if it is a great letter.[7]

Often the letter feels right once written and revised. It authentically expresses what the writer feels. Barriers to sending it melt away. The process of composing the letter, going through the stages to create impact, throwing out the debris, working through the feelings, and getting at the truth is so compelling that only rarely does the letter not eventually get sent. It may still be scary to send it, but the fear is generally manageable, especially when the writer uses techniques to control both the content and the response. One such technique is to start the letter with a statement of the writer's intent. For example, he may write: "I am sending this letter so that we can get rid of the barriers between us. I want to be closer." He may then become restrictive if the response to his letter shows that the recipient is not taking him seriously or is mistreating him all over again. Another technique is to end the letter by giving instructions as to what the writer wants the receiver to do: "Please write, don't call. This way it will be easier for me to think about your response." Giving instructions to the parents creates an automatic shift in power. The writer is saying what he requires, shifting the focus of the relationship. The parents have to deal with the writer's request and the writer's feelings and perceptions.

Letter writing reduces the vulnerability of the person trying out new behavior and increases his ability to stand back and analyze what the respondent does; at the same time, it helps the respondent get the distance necessary to be undefensive. For the letter recipient, the distance from the accuser that a letter provides can help prevent impulsive and defensive reactions. The fact that it is the written word rather than the spoken cry or scream gives the well-intentioned parent the opportunity to consider his feelings, his experience of the events or feelings referred to in the letter, and ultimately what seems to him to be true and what seems to be false. The responder as well as the writer has the letter to look at and ponder for future discussions. This means a future talk need not be based on misunderstandings because of strong emotions, which can easily prevent either party from communicating honestly. Not spoiling the chance to communicate in person becomes a crucial advantage of the letter home.

Honesty and openness do not ensure a good response. My new open behavior may not get treated with respect. I need to be prepared for a bad response. I need to try the new behavior for my own sake, not because I expect specific responses from someone else. People are extremely vulnerable when they try a new behavior for the first time. Preparatory work is important. The more safeguards that can be built in, the better the chances of establishing a solid foundation for change.

A caution is important here: Letters confronting abuse are obviously not appropriate to send when the recipient is homicidal, violent, psychotic, or psychopathic or in any way poses a physical threat to the writer. In less dangerous situations when the writer can't assume goodwill on the part of the recipient, the writer can protect herself from anticipated threats by building in a counter-threat technique. The writer can decide to send copies of her letter to everyone in the family and explain in her letter that she is sending copies because she is no longer willing to keep secrets. Or, she can give the parent fair warning that if the parent distorts what she says and communicates that distortion to the other family members, she will send copies of her letter to them. The writer can announce that she intends to break off a bad relationship and give instructions to cease all future contact unless certain conditions are met. She can stipulate that she no longer wants any relationship but wants to say why she has been avoiding the parent and why she feels the way she does.

If the writer writes her parents and honestly and openly expresses to them what she has always secretly blamed them for, she is freed up. Writing letters is less frequent in these days of easy phone access and electronic mail; its rarity makes letters all the more potent. If the writer's parent is not accustomed to getting letters that communicate real feelings and request real responses, the letter will grab attention. Having articulated her feelings, and knowing that the letter will get read and attended to if sent, the writer starts to gain additional perspective; she can start to see what she contributes to being treated badly or to not stopping the bad treatment before she even drops the letter in the mailbox.

2

Letters to Confront Problems

Dr. B., an attractive thirty-six-year-old professor, was in therapy for several years before she was referred to me. The oldest of four children and the only female, she grew up in poverty on a farm in Appalachia.

She worked with me for four years in individual and then in group therapy to undo the effects of the severe abuse she suffered from her father, brothers, and mother throughout her childhood. I assigned her the task of writing her father to confront him about his sexual abuse of her. Although I had been assigning letters in therapy for many years, she was the first client I asked to confront sexual abuse in a letter. When I saw the profound change writing this letter made in her life, I realized that writing such a letter was a far more potent agent of change than I had understood. Later she wrote to her dead mother. Writing was a way to express feelings that she initially found impossible to communicate in person. Once she wrote about "forbidden feelings," she could talk about them.

The feelings expressed in Dr. B.'s letter had been internally articulated for so many years that she wrote the first draft easily. She brought the letter into her therapy session the week after I assigned it. She was relieved to have written it and eager to send it. She felt especially good to be telling her father the real reason she dreaded contact with him. Writing the letter made her realize how absurd it was to feel guilty about not going home for the holidays. And although she had talked in therapy about the abuse she suffered growing up, she had never gone into such detail. Writing helped her integrate her trauma in a way that gave her perspective. For the first time, she could talk about the experiences and feelings without re-experiencing shame and guilt.

As you read her letter, notice the matter-of-fact tone. I learned later on to recognize this tone as a defense that protects the writer from fully feeling her outrage while it protects the parent from the full impact of the writer's feelings. If I had had more experience with letter therapy, I would have asked Dr. B. to rewrite the letter, putting in the feelings that she had left out. Note, too, that she imagines an exchange: She imagines her father's responses and tries to answer them. She reaches out to him, hoping that he will respond in kind. Her longing to get through to him and to transform their relationship is as palpable as her contained anger. In spite of this longing to connect with her father, Dr. B. is very specific about what she wants and what she does not want. Therefore, she can make an accurate assessment of her father's responses and know what to do with them.

Dear Dad,

I have been meaning to write to you or have a serious discussion with you for some time, but have continually put it off.

I've decided to now, however, since I'm aware that the biggest reason I'm not coming home for the holidays has to do with not wanting to be around you, at least not until I feel some issues are resolved.

I think you do not realize how damaging your sexual abuse of me as a child and teenager was. If you do, you have never acknowledged it and we have never really talked about it. I think I may have tried to let you know a few times that I was angry or disapproved, but you've never said much about it.

I'm enclosing an article on incest for you to read. While it doesn't cover a lot of things, I think it may help you understand some of the points I wish to make.

You exploited me tremendously, especially after mother died. You may tell yourself that because you never had intercourse per se with me, none of the rest of it counts. That's a lot of crap. It was bad enough that I had to grow up with an alcoholic mother who felt things were so bad she would kill herself. And then no mother at all. But then to have you constantly after me, feeling me up or trying to get in bed with me, or getting in bed and playing with my genitals, sticking your hands inside me, rubbing against me, trying to get me to jack you off, forever walking in on me when I was changing and telling me I was abnormal because I objected, and etc., etc., etc. It's all too much to go into here, but you know what you did. And I was about to go crazy, trying to find ways to get you to leave me alone, making excuses to stay up so you wouldn't get in my bed, trying not to let you get between me and a door, so I could always have a chance at escaping from you.

You may say to yourself, "Well, if you minded so much, how come you put up with it?" The reason I put up with it is because that's the way most kids are when they are six or seven. They're vulnerable to their parents and generally do what they're told. Especially timid kids like me. I was afraid of my own shadow for most of my childhood, because mother had been so strict. And when I got older and things got so much more frequent after mother died, I was simply too timid and scared to stand up for myself and tell you to go to hell. And when I did try to reason with you that it was wrong, you refused to listen. Didn't you ever once wonder why for years I lay there stiff in bed, not moving unless you moved me, like some kind of mannequin? Because I was scared to death and didn't have any idea how to protect myself. And what I learned from all of your "teaching" (seems like you once claimed to be teaching me about sex, so I wouldn't be frigid) was to hate sex and to hate and distrust men and, to a certain extent, to hate myself. And especially I learned to hate you, for putting me through the years of mental and physical torture.

In addition to my anger about being sexually exploited and molested, I am furious about how you raised me as a female child. Your ideas about women are seriously warped. You were forever sending the message that all women were "chippies" at heart and out for what they could get, that a woman can't make it in life without a man to "keep" her, and that I'd better shape up and learn how to please and exploit men, since I'd never make it on my own. As you so frequently and succinctly put it, "Even the garbage-man wouldn't have you," since I re-fused to try to be sexy and submissive with men (or not enough to please you, anyway). I realize your experience with your girlfriends generally confirms this negative view of women, since you only pick out women who play the game the way you do, and distort what you see of women who don't. I don't know why you hate women . . . maybe you're just afraid of them. I really don't know and at this point I don't much care. But I do know that your whole approach to women is destructive and devaluing.

I have protected you for years, even after I found out I could have had you thrown in jail (which was what finally gave me the guts at age seventeen to tell you to keep your hands off me) . . . but I couldn't see trading a known hell for an unknown one. The best I felt I could do was avoid you as much as possible and arrange to start fights with you, because I knew if you were mad at me, you'd leave me alone sexually. So when you tell yourself I was a "difficult" teenager, be aware that you were the cause of it.

Why, you are probably asking yourself, am I so angry about something that happened years ago? First, you have never acknowledged that you did anything at all wrong. You have never apologized for the damage you have done to me and my life. I have had to spend most of my adult years in and out of psychotherapy, trying to straighten out the damage you did. Between you and mother, it is a miracle I'm not nuts. When I have shared with people what my life at home was like, they are usually horrified and amazed that I have managed to survive as sane as I am. Unfortunately for me, I am still having difficulty relating to men without my anger at you interfering. And I have been periodically suicidal, which is part your doing, although partly mother's, too. If you'll read the article I've enclosed, you'll find that extremely low self-esteem and suicidal thoughts are one of the common outcomes for the incest victim. I even considered becoming a prostitute during my teens (another common result for the victim), only I was too timid and felt I wasn't pretty enough (something which you also had a part in).

While I have managed to straighten out a lot of the problems my upbringing has caused, I have not managed to get over the anger and bitterness I feel toward you. Usually I have ignored my feelings and suppressed them, thinking it wasn't worth the hassle to make waves and knowing no one else in the family would understand if I did, since they wouldn't understand what I was so angry about. But I'm discovering that by not getting these issues out in the open, I am only making life more difficult for me, while you go on oblivious to how I feel and what you've done. It has been hard for me to confront you openly with these things at home, because the boys did not know about them (except John, a little bit) and I've worried about how they would take it. But I told Frank a little about it last spring and told Charlie recently and plan to send each of the boys a copy of this letter, because I want them to know why I resent you so. The reason I am not coming home for Christmas this year is that I don't plan to go through any more visits with you, pretending like everything is fine, when it's not. It's too much strain on me.

So what do I want? I would like a sincere apology from you and acknowledgment that what you did was wrong. I would like you to see a shrink and try to learn about how it is you could almost destroy your own child and either not be aware of it or not care you were doing it. I would like you to learn why you can't relate to women in a healthy way and to try to change it. And if you can't, I don't ever want to hear about you and your women and your sex life again or to have to listen to derogatory comments about women or about me.

I do not know if it is possible for us to have any kind of relationship in the future. I, for one, am not willing to try to work anything out with you without a third-party mediator present, such as my therapist or some other trained mental health professional. If you can't or won't make the changes I think are necessary, then I need to stay away from you. You have done enough damage to me already.

In any case, I do not believe you are to be trusted around female children. I am glad you are not especially close to any of the female grandchildren, as you are not to be trusted. I have not seen any evidence that you've changed, and that you wouldn't molest another child, given sufficient opportunity.

If you care to respond to this letter, please do it in writing. I don't plan to talk to you by phone or without someone else present who understands what the situation is. And if you choose not to respond and ignore what I say, then I expect I will not be seeing you again. I refuse to go through the rest of my life pretending nothing ever happened.

B.

The practice afforded by writing openly and bravely, saying what you have never said before, is the beginning of building a skill. This trial behavior gives the writer a sense of mastery. With a sense of mastery comes a renewed sense of possibilities and empowerment.[1]

Sending the letter brings it out of the realm of trial and practice and into the realm of responsibility. The writer can take ownership of her feelings and thoughts, get a real reaction, and take responsibility for dealing with that reaction.

In her letter to her father, Dr. B. clearly has empathy for herself as a child who did not stop her father's sexual abuse earlier. As she wrote, she became aware that she could have stopped her father's abuse before she actually did. Knowing that she had had more power than she had given herself credit for became an important spur to action. It was this awareness that allowed her to immediately and irrevocably cut her father off when in his response letter he admitted to the incest while denying that it was abusive—after all, he said, he had given her special gifts for submitting to sex with him.

Confronting her father and giving up hope about the possibility of working out a viable relationship with him produced a dramatic change in her. Because she was no longer in contact with him, she was no longer subjecting herself to his emotional abuse. She could then begin to put his sexual abuse of her (and the shame, guilt, and rage she felt about it) in the past, where it belonged. Before writing this letter she constantly criticized and berated herself, clawed at her skin, and even attempted suicide. She set herself up to be abused by others emotionally and sexually. After writing the letter she rarely abused herself, and she no longer let anyone else abuse her.

About six months later, Dr. B. began to focus on her mother in therapy in a way she had never before been able to do. She decided to write a letter to her dead mother.

Mother,

I am angry at you for being a drunk, and refusing to do anything about it.

I am angry at you for feeling so sorry for yourself all the time, instead of doing something about what you were angry about.

I am angry about your unwillingness to go to anyone (meaning professionals) for help with your problems.

I am angry about your failure to stand up for yourself with the old man.

I am angry at you for helping to make my childhood miserable.

I am angry at you for copping out and leaving me to cope with the old man by myself.

I am angry at you for embarrassing me by killing yourself.

I'm angry about the way you risked our lives (the children) by driving drunk.

I'm angry about your inflexibility and impatience in parenting — you were too strict and had unreasonable expectations.

I'm angry about your threats to give us all to the orphanage.

I'm angry about your bad temper and being slapped in the face when you lost your temper.

I'm angry at you for not protecting me better, by letting me play on dangerous machinery which damaged my foot forever.

I'm angry at you for burdening me with your hours of self-pity, and using me as a captive audience.

I'm angry that you helped me think I was a bad person, by your critical attitude.

I'm angry at you for making me afraid when you got drunk, by hurting my brothers or acting weird.

I'm angry at you for generally being a lousy parent to me.

I'm angry at you for treating me as competition for the old man rather than as his daughter.

B.

Dr. B. had so concentrated her feelings on the incest and her father's abuse of her that she had not fully understood her mother's role in the abuse she suffered or the effect of her mother's suicide on the family. Not until she got free of her father could she understand and integrate her feelings about her mother. Generally in families where one parent is the blatant abuser, the other parent is colluding—either overtly by helping set up the child to be abused or subtly by denying the abuse and giving the child the message that she should also deny it. This subtle collusion sometimes occurs because the parent, like the child, is victimized by the abusive parent and denies the abuse to herself. This parent then models victimization behavior to the child. Until she started writing to her mother, Dr. B. was not aware of how much rage she felt toward her. In this letter, Dr. B. literally wrote out her rage.

Writing a letter to her father and then to her dead mother freed Dr. B. to be straightforward instead of appeasing in her daily life. She became involved in a loving relationship and lived with her lover for the rest of her life. When she discovered she was dying of cancer after having worked so hard to become happy and fulfilled, she used her new assertive skills to prevent the medical system from mistreating her, even when she was weak and scared. She fired several doctors before she found a doctor she respected. On a few occasions, she needed to confront her doctor with feelings that were especially difficult for her, so she used her letter-writing skills to assert herself.

Experimental research shows that writing about upsetting or traumatic events that have been kept secret can create beneficial change.[2] In their 1988 article, Pennebaker, Kiecolt-Glaser, and R. Glaser, studying the effect of written expression on the immune system found that the group of college students who were instructed to write about "the most traumatic and upsetting experiences of your entire life" reported feeling happier than they were before the writing experience; their immune functions improved and they had fewer visits to the student health center. The other group, who were instructed to write on an assigned neutral topic, describing "specific objects or events in detail without discussing your own thoughts or feelings," reported feeling the same as they had before the experiment; their immune functions showed no improvement, and there was no change in the number of visits they made to the health center.[3]

Pennebaker and Sussman theorize that when we hold back thoughts and feelings associated with an important event, we fail to translate the event into language and therefore fail to understand or assimilate the event and so are unable to put it behind us:

> Confiding about traumatic experience . . . appears to have positive physical and psychological effects in the long run.[4]
>
> The act of inhibiting ongoing behavior, emotions, and thoughts requires physiological work. . . . In our view, inhibition can be viewed as a source of stress that, over time, is cumulative and increases the probability of disease. Indeed, in the immune study discussed above, we found that those people who wrote about things that they reported wanting to have told others about (but had not) showed the most dramatic improvements in immune system functioning.[5]

If inhibiting feelings and thoughts about upsetting events is stressful and makes the body work in ways that have negative emotional and physical effects, we can expect disclosing these feelings and thoughts to be healthy. I wonder what would have been the effect on Dr. B.'s physical health had she written her letters and experienced the changes they brought to her life when she was in her twenties instead of her late thirties. I have no doubt that she lived longer than she would have otherwise because of her open and assertive letters to her doctor and to me throughout the course of her cancer, and because of her loving relationship with her partner. She outlived her doctor's predictions of her probable life expectancy by many years.

In his 1989 study on the effect of support groups on patients with metastatic breast cancer, David Spiegel, a professor of psychiatry and behavioral medicine at Stanford University, reported that cancer patients in support groups lived twice as long as control cancer patients who were not in support groups but received the same medical treatment. These groups were not psychotherapy groups. Spiegel merely facilitated open expression of thoughts, feelings, and experiences related to the patients' cancer.[6]

The research demonstrates in an experimental and verifiable way what I and other therapists and clients have discovered by sorting through what does and does not work in therapy: Articulating feelings, whether in conversation or in a letter, can help people caught in self-defeating patterns get out of them.

3

Changing the Pattern

Behavior that is self-defeating is repetitive and patterned, whereas healthy behavior tends to be spontaneous and flexible. To be at an impasse is to be caught in a particular rigid pattern. For example, Dr. B. kept getting involved in relationships with authority figures who were similar to her parents. She picked male authority figures who would become inappropriately sexual with her and female authority figures who would criticize her and ultimately abandon her. Each time she would end up feeling angry and violated.

When Dr. B. let go of her old self-image as a person who deserved to be used and discarded, she stopped getting involved in abusive relationships. Because she was no longer angry and victimized, her responses were no longer predictable.

Patterns of self-defeating behavior originate as early attempts at a solution to early problems; it is a solution in the sense that it is a defense that allowed the person to avoid or not feel the full, painful impact of the problem—for example, not to feel power-less in the face of superior, abusive power. Several of the writers whose letters appear in *Letters Home* solved the problem of the painful feelings they experienced when their parents undermined their accomplishments and punished their successes by under-mining themselves before their parents had the chance. This put them in control and lessened their sense of surprise and betrayal, thereby lessening their pain. Because it has served as protection in the past, this kind of solution is not likely to be dropped, even though the problem may no longer exist and even though it is not really a solution.

We repeat the past by continuing to set up the same pattern, or in Eric Berne's language, script (as in the script of a play), with new characters.[1] This is what Freud called repetition compul-sion.[2] We pick a friend or partner who abuses us the same way our parents did, or seduces us the same way, or neglects us the same way. We stay stuck in the same place so that our world is at least familiar and predictable.

This poor choosing is not as self-destructively motivated as it might seem. Each time we pick the parent replica or train the new significant other to be our "bad" parent, we not only re-create the old conflict, we also create the opportunity or possibil-ity that this time we can produce a different outcome.[3]

I believe that since we and our parents or significant others set up the original script or pattern for our lives, we will stay mired in the past, re-creating the past, if we do not confront our feelings about our parents. But if we still believe that our parents or par-ent replicas will change "if only we please them by behaving the right way," or "if only we make ourselves understood by express-ing ourselves better," then we are immobilized. We have all the old feelings and thoughts and no new solutions. The cast of char-acters may be new, but the roles and outcome stay the same. And although this is devastatingly disappointing and often enraging, it is reassuringly and even deliciously familiar.

After a period of time we may internalize the conflict. We do not even need real others to represent the parent. We internalize the bad parent and abuse ourselves the way they abused us (in extreme cases), or treat ourselves badly or neglectfully the way they treated us badly or neglectfully.

The fact that we pick and train others to play unresolved parental roles is what makes the confrontation with the parent so pivotal for change. Even writing letters to dead or near-dead parents, as in Dr. B.'s letter to her dead mother, or Nancy's letter to her mother (Chapter 8), which she read while her mother was in a coma, can shatter old myths and change old scripts. If we change our relationship with our parent, our relationship to others also changes. If writing the confrontation feels safe enough to ensure that this essential step is taken, then writing becomes an invaluable tool for change.

When we write such a letter, we may discover that we have to change our view of our parents and ourselves, or we may confirm our view of our parents, pronounce them hopeless, and move away from futile efforts to get them to acknowledge some reality about us or our life with them, as Dr. B. did as a result of writing to her father.

Many of our clients grew up being told directly or indirectly that they were selfish, stupid, incompetent, powerless, unattractive, or, more generically, bad people. Since their parents or significant others are often the source of these beliefs, they try throwing off these limiting self-concepts by trying to change their parents' views of them. They are stuck with their destructive negative self-concept as long as they need acknowledgment from their parents that they are not bad or stupid. To change their powerful self-beliefs, they need to realize what it is they believe about themselves and how they came to believe it. Until they deal with the conflicts with the parent figures or parent substitutes, they cannot understand that they are giving away the power to define themselves. Without this power, they remain locked in a struggle with their parents that leaves them irresponsible—waiting and hoping for their parents to change before they will change.

Writing a letter home, forcing yourself to articulate and back up your feelings with specific examples, can help sort out distortions. Sometimes writing a letter makes clear what benefits you get from staying enmeshed with your parents.

Often the writer expects that the response he gets will expose the extent to which the recipient is unwilling to change. Often it does just that. But the letter-writing process can also expose the writer's unwillingness to change, and it can help him understand how and why he is unwilling to change. It is hard to write the letter and not come to the realization that you often get into conflicts with others similar to the conflicts you are in with your parents. And then it is hard to deny that you get a payoff by collecting the same feelings about yourself from other people that you did from your parents. You may realize, for example, that what you are saying to your mother in the letter, what you are angry or sad about, is the same thing you are feeling but afraid to express in your relationship with your spouse, girlfriend, boss, or best friend. Writing to a parent or significant other about the past can force the writer to face the fact that he is repeating an old pattern with significant others in his current life. If you think that the problem is your parents', not yours, there may be little you can do except get out of their way. But if you know that you participate in the pattern because you see that you get involved with significant others in the same harmful way, then there is the chance to change the pattern by changing yourself.

Dr. B. became involved in a sexual relationship with her married teacher, who ignored her feelings but rewarded her in ways similar to the ways in which her father had rewarded her. He made her feel special compared to his other students. She collected the same feelings about herself and the world that she did when she was sexually abused by her father. At home she had felt special compared to her mother and brothers. As in the past, she knew she had a dirty secret that was her fault; she felt ignored at the same time she felt she was given unfair attention, and she felt hopeless. But she was "reassured" that the world was predictable, though rotten, and that she would always be victimized by men.

If the writer can move from an impasse with parents or significant others, either by cutting off a hopeless or abusive relationship or by changing it into a healthy one, she can set the stage for new healthy relationships. For Dr. B., the insights she got from writing confronting letters to her father and to her mother, and the resolution of the conflict with her father that her letter to him made possible, released her from her abusive pattern with male (and female) authority figures. She no longer believed that she deserved to be mistreated. She no longer repeated the old incestuous script, as she had with her teacher.

PART II

The Writing Process

Change is not made without inconvenience
even from worse to better.

— RICHARD HOOKER

4

Gathering Information

A letter writer can ask for information that can clarify misunderstandings, unearth secrets, and dispel myths. Often, though, the mere request for information in a family that is full of secrets brings on defensive attacks.

Gena began therapy, to a large extent, because she would fly into rages and hit her child. This mortified her. She had been regularly and brutally beaten by her alcoholic father while her mother watched. The beatings were witnessed and not in dispute. Her requests for information came as a result of her dissociative behavior and because her memories, behavior, and diagnostic testing indicated the possibility that she had been sexually abused as well. We told her that although it would be helpful if she could find out what did or did not happen, it was not critical for her therapy since we already knew she was abused and mistreated. Searching for specific information can be enlightening and can help integrate the experiences so that they are less damaging.

Sometimes, however, the searcher gets so caught up in her search and the reactions to it that she is distracted from the hard work of making changes. Sometimes the circumstances are such that the information is unknowable.

Gena wrote her mother asking her which other family members were with her when she was little and what her mother remembered about how they had treated her. Her mother responded angrily and defensively. Gena wrote the following response to her mother's letter:

Dear Mom,

I wanted to clear up a few misperceptions in your letter. You said in your letter that I am "extremely disturbed" and have "no peace of mind" because of my efforts to uncover the source of my possible sexual abuse . . . at this point in my life, I am probably the most assured and most at peace with myself that I have ever been. I am angry that as a young child I was beaten and exposed to a home environment which was unloving and brutal. I am sad for the little girl that had to endure that situation.

I no longer have the problem of unfulfilling friendships. I have friends of almost twenty years. . . . When I was younger . . . I was extremely distrustful of getting close to anyone because the people with whom I was the closest (you, Dad, Grandpa, and Grandma) were brutal, unprotective, and untrustworthy. I evolved a protective pattern: when I would get close to a person, rather than let a relationship evolve to the point of abuse as I assumed it would, I would take things into my own hands and push the person away before they could do it to me.

Now . . . I have the ability to make a conscious choice of who to trust and with whom to be friends and even colleagues. I avoid people who try to deny my feelings, who are hypercrit-

ical, and those who out of their own insecurities and low self-esteem try to poison me against other people. . . .

Finally, in your letter you suggested that you are a casualty—one of those with whom I am through. I have reached out in the past five or six years to try to establish a better relationship with you. And while I have the capacity to understand and even forgive at some level your abuse and your unwillingness to protect me against the abuse of others, it's not possible to forgive someone who seems unable to acknowledge their role and responsibility.

Gena

The attempt to gather information ended up generating a series of letters between Gena and her mother. Gena finally wrote a confronting letter regarding her mother's role in allowing her father to physically abuse her. And although her mother still responded defensively, the dialogue that opened up could not have been predicted from her mother's attacking response to Gena's initial request for information.

Her mother's later letters showed some desire to respond to Gena. Nevertheless, they were confusing and unsatisfactory. I asked Gena to diagram one of her mother's letters with a line-by-line analysis, so that she could understand what her mother did that was so disconcerting and infuriating. Gena's analysis was so clear and so helpful to her that she decided to send it to her mother.

Dear Mom,

Thank you for your last few letters that show an openness and eagerness to hear what I have to say. What I want to do in this letter is further our process of communication by sharing with you . . . a pattern that is preventing me from feeling you are responding to my concerns.

The pattern is this: (1) you begin to move toward acknowledging your role in the suffering of my childhood, but then, and it seems almost unconscious, you (2) shift gears and negate or backtrack from where you initially seem to be heading.

Here's a sample paragraph from your latest letter:

"I have never forgiven myself for all that you suffered. If I sometimes seemed distant, and cold as you mention I seemed to you—it wasn't being done due to you—but because I felt guilty about speaking out when you were 'hurting' and I was a part of the cause of it. I didn't deserve to offer you help or advice and perhaps cause you more grief."

I've put your words in quotes and my questions and response in . . . parenthesis.

"I have never forgiven myself for all that you suffered."
(Here is where you acknowledge you have something for which to be forgiven and that it has something to do with my suffering. For what do you need to be forgiven?)

"If I sometimes seemed distant, and cold as you mention I seemed to you—it wasn't being done to you." (This does not make sense since it was being done to me.) "But because I felt guilty about speaking out when you were hurting and I was part of the cause of it." (How were you "part of the cause" of it? Where did your guilty feeling come from?)

"I didn't deserve to offer help or advice" (What do you mean by you "didn't deserve to offer help"?)

"and perhaps cause you more grief." (It's not clear to me how
you would have caused me more grief. Normally a parent tries
to console their child when something bad has happened.)

. . . You often at first seem truly contrite, but then you switch
gears, obfuscate, and I end up feeling that you are once again
relieving yourself of any responsibility for what happened to
me when Dad was around. You seem incapable of acknowl-
edging your role in allowing the abuse to go on. You never say
that you did something wrong. You offer excuses.
   I look forward to . . . keeping a dialogue going.

                                                    Gena

Her mother's next letter indicated that she understood she was
not responding appropriately to Gena. She said she did not know
how to respond better and as a result had started individual psychotherapy. She invited Gena to come to a future session and to
get together to talk. Several months after her mother started
therapy, Gena received an open and heartfelt letter from her
mother clearly demonstrating that she could take responsibility
for her role in Gena's abuse. Gena responded with the following
letter:

Dear Mom,
   Thank you very much for your letter. You were very respon-
sive to my concerns by acknowledging the role that you played
in not protecting me from Father's abuse and by sharing the
guilt that you feel.
   I am feeling much more trusting of you and I look forward
to getting together with you. One idea that Drew and I had, af-
ter reading the article you sent a while ago on Cumberland

*County, is meeting you there once the weather gets better to do
some bird and nature watching. What do you think?*

*I am sure that things will be a little awkward between us at
first, but I am committed to making our visit a good one. I
know that there are things that each of us individually does
that rubs the other wrong. I sometimes am too quick to anger
and too forceful in my response. At other times I become distant and withdraw rather than engage in a conversation that
could prove difficult. Over the two and one-half years that we
have been writing I have mentioned things you do that set me
off such as your becoming cold and distant or starting to cry
when you are angry or focusing too much on possible negative
consequences. I feel that we have built the basis for good discussions including being able to tell each other when our behaviors become annoying and counterproductive. . . .*

Love,

Gena

....

For Meg, the idea of voicing a criticism to her parents was un-
thinkable. Even asking for information that might cause her parents to be uncomfortable was frightening.

In Meg's family, feelings, especially angry ones, were taboo.
Her father was absent much of the time, and when he was home
he was distant. Her mother expected both her one natural child
and all her adopted children (Meg was adopted at age two) to feel
what she felt, want what she wanted, and do what she told them
to do. Meg came into therapy denying all negative feelings. She
gradually became aware of how angry she was, how little she expected from others, and how much she gave to them.

She married a man she took care of, who gave her very little in
return. Like her mother, he expected her to be his clone and mir-

ror his needs. When they had children, he manipulated them and denied their feelings. She felt moved to protect her children in ways she had never been moved to protect herself. She insisted that her husband become involved in individual therapy and then in couples therapy. He complied. His only motivation to change was his fear that Meg would leave him. This was not enough motivation to sustain genuine change.

Meg stayed in the relationship a few more years, working hard in therapy and hoping her husband would change. But over time she recognized that her relationship with him would never be fulfilling and ultimately she decided to divorce him.

Meg had always been afraid to ask her mother for information about her birth mother. Now she had the strength to request this information. When Meg asked her mother questions about her birth mother in a telephone conversation, her mother responded as if Meg was attacking her. It was this response to her request for information that finally gave Meg the impetus to deal with her feelings about her mother. The letter she wrote was the first communication to her mother in which she expressed critical feelings. Although her mother did send the requested adoption information, she ignored Meg's confrontation. She sent a birthday card, the gist of which was, You are being hateful but we love you anyway. Here is Meg's "hateful" letter:

Dear Mom,

I am writing to respond to your letter and our phone conversation regarding adoption. You said you could not understand why your adopted children were so curious about our birth histories because you never were. When I asked if you had been adopted, you said, "No." Clearly you are unable to put yourself in my place and imagine that I would be curious and want some information. It saddens and disappoints me to see how totally lacking in empathy you are. Furthermore, it alarms me that you choose to feel "hurt and shocked" that I would be searching for information. And you choose to take it personally, as if it has anything to do with you. Of course, adopted kids are curious about their histories. It is normal. It is not normal for a parent to respond with hurt and shock if a child has a need different from theirs.

. . . You wrote that you "tried to love" me and did what you could to rear me "along with all the others." Well, unfortunately you "tried" but failed. Making me feel like a burden "along with all the others" doesn't show love. Witholding empathy doesn't show love and keeping secrets doesn't either. Speaking of secrets, as for Margie being gay, that is her need and her choice. I care about her and accept her for who she is, not who I want her to be. And telling Dad isn't going to kill him off. You just said that to manipulate Margie into keeping her life a secret. I doubt whether he'll care one way or the other.

And finally, as for your denial of anger, Mom, get real. You are furious every time that any of us are or do things you don't want. Real love is loving and encouraging someone to do what is right for them. I want you to know that I'm angry at you about the things I listed here. Please think over what I've said . . . before you answer. I am interested in a real dialogue.

Meg

After several more letter exchanges, Meg gave up on her mother. She wrote to her father and included the packet of correspondence with her mother. Initially her father's response was supportive. He agreed with much of what Meg said about her mother and acknowledged that his wife was mean and hard to live with. He told Meg that he was very depressed. But after another letter exchange between Meg and her mother, in which her mother was very angry and defensive, her father stopped writing. Meg called him and during the conversation he backtracked. He then wrote advising her to follow his philosophy: Forget her anger, attend to only the positives in life, and make peace with her mother. This inspired Meg to write the following letter:

Dear Dad,

I am sad that you can't understand and acknowledge my feelings. It was so helpful when you agreed that Mom is "mean as dirt" and when you said you know she digs into people. You are clearly aware that her remarks are offensive and hurtful. However, your denial of my right to feel angry and your insistence that people should only attend to the positive have badly affected my life. I didn't fight back when people close to me were mean and hurtful and I had to live with the pain by myself because I didn't think I could tell anyone about it. Telling you my feelings has not been a satisfying experience because of your warped philosophy that says not to feel any anger. I am disappointed that you couldn't take better care of yourself or me. If you had allowed yourself to be angry and confront Mom's destructive criticism I don't think you would be so depressed today. . . . I regret the years I wasted trying to please Mom, who was never satisfied, only competitive, about my accomplishments. It would have helped me so much if you had acknowledged my intelligence and creativity. It would have helped even more if you had protected yourself and me and not thrown me to the wolf to avoid making things worse for you.

Meg

Gena's initial written request for information (not reprinted here) and Meg's initial telephone request for information were not particularly confrontational. But because of the disappointing responses their requests elicited, they ended up writing confrontational letters that they had not originally intended to write. This led to unchartered territory, a more realistic appraisal of what kind of relationship with their parents was and was not possible, and eventually to profound changes in their relationships with their parents.

Although Gena never found the answers to her questions regarding possible sexual abuse, that became less important to her as she resolved other issues. Gena has opened up new possibilities for closeness with her mother. Meg did obtain the information she wanted but was unable to resolve any of the issues she had with her parents. She has closed off an unsatisfying and destructive relationship with her mother. Her relationship with her father will most likely revert to the distant relationship they had before Meg's letters home. She is no longer connected to either of her parents by rage and frustrated hope.

The work Gena and Meg did to change their own lives had a profound effect on the next generation. Gena stopped abusing her son. Meg no longer denied her own or her children's feelings, and she helped her children deal with their father when he tried to deny their feelings.

5

Writing Drafts
and Getting Feedback

O ne of the main advantages of writing a letter to a significant
other is that the writer can write consecutive drafts and get
feedback each time on what stands in the way of communicating
effectively. Feedback needs to come from whomever the writer
trusts to be honest, critical, and supportive. As with any form of
writing, a letter can be worked on, revised, put aside, reread, and
critiqued until the writer is saying what he wants to say in a way
that has the most chance of getting through and is least likely to
set him up to get clobbered.

First drafts often reveal the writer's lingering fear of having an
impact. Feedback on these drafts is crucial. Especially important
is feedback on what I call "take-aways," devices that dampen the
factual or emotional impact of the letter. Recognizing them can
make the writer aware of his fear of making an impact and of the
methods he uses to decrease impact. Not surprisingly, the way a

writer takes away his potency in a letter is often parallel to the way he does it in person.

Often a writer hides his feelings using several take-away techniques at once to avoid confronting his parent about the major issues. The most common methods used to take away from a letter's impact are psychobabbling (writing psychological jargon that is platitudinous or even meaningless and/or using psychological terms or assumptions that the recipient of the letter will not understand), positioning as a victim by trying to elicit pity or guilt, rushing to rescue or reassure the letter recipient, citing potent examples to illustrate an important point but with bland affect, citing trivial examples to illustrate an important point, and explaining or teaching in a pedantic way.

A writer can reduce the impact of his letter by the way he uses language. When a letter is filled with psychobabble, it either fails to communicate or alienates the reader before he can consider the content. It alienates because it is either jargon or such special language that it excludes the reader. When Dave wrote his first draft, it was filled with long Germanic sentences explaining and analyzing his own or his parents' dynamics; he used phrases such as "passive-aggressive maneuvers." When he revised his letter, the assignment to eliminate this special language and to write as if he were a smart ten-year-old helped him to write directly and simply about his feelings. His revised letters are in Chapter 14.

It is hard to take the writer who starts with a tone of victimization seriously. The parent who receives a letter with this tone can easily decide that the writer's views are colored by her depression and therefore discount the entire letter. In the beginning of Ellen's first draft to her father she positioned herself as pitiful victim:

I have so much pain from growing up in your house that there are times I just don't want to live anymore. Sometimes I feel as if I can't take another breath. Sometimes my life seems like an endless struggle that isn't worth it.

When Ellen revised her letter, she eliminated the victim tone as well as her veiled suicide threat. Her powerful revised letter appears in Chapter 17.

In the first draft of her letter to her mother, Dottie minimized her impact by too many reassuring "I love you" statements. When she saw the difference in impact with and without the sappy phrases, she took them out. But when she received a response letter in which her mother acknowledged her feelings, she was so grateful that in the draft of her answer to her mother she again minimized her impact, this time in a subtler way than she had in her first letter:

For me, the biggest part of the healing process was in my letter and the forgiving came with your letter. I know you feel badly about your part in our past, and I hope you will take the guilt and stuff it in a trash bag and throw it out of the house. I think it will just get in the way. I meant what I said about us both wanting the same thing from each other. The love is already there but the sharing and learning about each other will just take practice. I'm looking forward to that.

This apology for having had impact that could cause her mother distress is a mistake common to letter writers as well as others who assert themselves, maybe for the first time, have an impact, and then feel so uncomfortable with their power that they try to take the impact away. After getting feedback Dottie rewrote with no rescue attempt and no apology:

I know you feel guilty and I think that's good if it motivates a change in your behavior with me. It isn't good if it keeps you focused on you rather than on me.

In this revision, Dottie does not try to make her mother feel better. This is important because if her mother takes Dottie seriously her mother will feel some pain. This bad feeling, if it is genuine, can inspire her to reevaluate her relationship with her daughter and to examine what she needs to change in her behavior if she is to have a better relationship. Dottie's complete revised letter appears in Chapter 13.

Even when the content is powerful, giving terrible specifics of emotional, sexual, or physical abuse in a bland tone makes the abuse sound matter-of-fact or harmless. As I mentioned earlier, Dr. B.'s letter to her father (in Chapter 2) had an anesthetized quality. When terrible things are described, as in Dr. B.'s letter, but reading about them does not make your blood curdle, you know the writer is reducing her potency by making the abusive behavior seem innocuous so that she does not have to be taken seriously.

When the writer gives specifics that are trivial, the recipient(s) can discount everything the writer has to say. The writer may illustrate her point with some slight that the parent can legitimately respond to by claiming that the writer wants the parent to be perfect. The parent can easily discount the underlying point because the example is inconsequential. In this way, the writer guarantees that she will be discounted and that she and her parents will not have to face or have feelings about the real issues.

Cindy, whose letters appear in Chapter 10, was challenged by her group when she cited a trivial example that she planned to include in her letter. To illustrate how her parents constantly criticized her looks, she said her mother nagged her about her skin.

Her group told her that this was typical mother stuff and asked for other examples. When Cindy told us her mother made fun of her mouth by saying it was so big it looked like Martha Raye's and told Cindy she took after the ugly side of the family and that her father called her "four eyes" and "crip," she burst into tears. When talking about the trivial example, she showed no emotion. Cindy realized that she had not planned to include real examples in her letter because she was protecting herself from the painful feelings that these incidents elicited. She was also protecting herself from the negative response she anticipated if her letter had a real impact on her parents. In her final draft she has, for the most part, been successful at weeding out trivial examples.

It is not difficult to spot the use of trivial examples that portray the parents as ordinary people when, in fact, the parents are emotionally and/or physically abusive. Tina's first draft is a dramatic example. Her father died a few months before she wrote it. Keep in mind as you read this section of her draft letter that Tina's father was emotionally abusive to everyone in the family. There is increasing evidence that he was also physically abusive to the point of damaging his children (numerous incidents of broken arms, legs, and jaws were never explained) and very possibly sexually abusive. When Tina asked about her damaged jaw, she was told that she fell off a swing, but she has no memory of this event. The "accident" left her with severe, still visible damage to her face, which was not treated at the time. One of her brothers broke an arm under mysterious circumstances, and though he screamed in pain his father told him to get over it. It was not until several days later that he was taken to the hospital. A sister supposedly fell down the basement steps, but she thinks she was pushed. As more information emerges, it appears that when the girls were very young their father may have sexually abused them. Tina and one of her older sisters (each unbeknownst to the other) began to deal with this possibility in their therapy. At this point it is not possible or even necessary to find out. Her mother is so clinically disturbed that she is unreliable, even if she knew what happened when her children were toddlers. We do know that Tina's mother did not stand up for the children against her tyrannical husband.

Even when she was an adult with her own children, Tina's father habitually screamed at her, publicly berating her when he could not get his way. When she became upset during one of his barrages, he would become sweet and seductive.

In the first few paragraphs of her draft letter, it is as if Tina only wants to balance the slightly biased picture of her father that the family has promoted. It is hard to tell from this draft that she is enraged at her father for the damage he has done to her, her mother, and the other children. Here are the first two paragraphs:

> *Dear Martha, Tom, Marilyn, and Mom,*
>
> *Everyone has spent much time and effort eulogizing Dad and making note of all his accomplishments serving the people of Watertown. I think it is necessary to also look at the other side of him and keep him in perspective.*
>
> *Dad was a strong, controlling and very manipulative person. He was gone, away from home and us more than he was with us! He had a way of distorting our perceptions when they did not coincide with his and when he did not want to admit that he was wrong. He would not take "no" for an answer or tolerate differing opinions than his. He refused to deal with his feelings or anyone else's in our family, by just ignoring whatever was happening.*

Tina knows the art of understatement. What she says in these paragraphs is all true; it just does not go far enough. After getting feedback, she decided she should start over, this time writing to her dead father to get at her real feelings. She knew this would help make the letter rawer and truer. Already her work on the draft and the feedback she received about her minimizing have helped her deal with an abusive employee who reminds her of her father.

It was at least five months before Tina reluctantly returned to the task of writing her dead father. She reported in group that as soon as she began writing about her anger, her father appeared in fantasy "on her left shoulder." In a seductive voice he told her she was mistaken about him. He said he had been a good father. This stopped her cold and she immediately "forgot" what she had been feeling. When we asked whether anyone else appeared to her while she was writing to her father, she said yes. Tina explained that there were two Tinas, one she called Healthy Tina and the other she called Unhealthy Tina. Unhealthy Tina showed up as soon as she started writing about her negative feelings. She reported that she had experienced this split ever since she could remember. She recognized that the fear she felt when she was writing about her anger at her father brought on the "switch," as she called it, to Unhealthy Tina. Unhealthy Tina used logic to talk Healthy Tina out of her feelings and was generally successful. In several years of individual and group therapy, Tina had never before told us about this splitting off of herself into two Tinas. It did not strike her as unusual, since the two Tinas had been with her ever since she could remember.

The real significance of Tina's revelation was not the change of her diagnosis to multiple personality disorder but that she was able to tell us about this private inner experience. Without the stimulus of the letter and Tina's description of how and in what way writing her second draft without the "take-aways" was so torturous for her, we may never have discovered this splitting of herself into two. This discovery gave further credence to the hypothesis that Tina experienced early sexual abuse because, as multiple personality disorder expert Dr. Ronald Batson puts it, "the most commonly encountered childhood experience linked to the formation of MPD appears to be repetitive sexual violation, usually coupled with violence." This dissociative response to abusive subordination is thought to occur only "before the age of six to eight when the consolidation of a cohesive sense of self is still in flux."[1] Because we now knew about the two Tinas we could help her understand and integrate the different parts of herself in a deeper way than we had previously.

....

Edward wrote a first draft in which he minimized and blunted his angry feelings toward his father and took the role of the sympathetic teacher with some psychobabble thrown in. The teaching technique Edward uses in his first draft, which has the flavor of "if you learn and understand this it will be good for you," is often employed by a writer who is furious—enraged because he anticipates that no matter how he expresses himself the parent will not acknowledge the legitimacy of what he is saying and will instead threaten or attack him. In addition to teaching, Edward shared the blame:

> *One of the traits that you and I have that I would most like to change is how mean and hurtful we can be toward people.*

He then blamed his father's bad behavior on his father's mother and concluded:

> *I do know if you had a choice and knew what to do, you would make it different. I think you had a lousy teacher and I feel terrible about how things are between Grandma and you. I'm*

sorry for both you and me that she taught you and you taught me some messages that have screwed up our ability to be more open and honest with each other.

He further excused his dad by saying:

I know you feel very strongly about your family. It just gets missed. . . . It's not an easy thing to do when you've not been taught these things at an early age and given the opportunity to practice. You and I can both change things from here on just by realizing that it's not good for anyone, including ourselves, to deny these wonderful feelings to people we care about.

This draft letter was an important learning experience for Edward because it helped him realize the ways he was like his father and the ways he made himself powerless. It was essential for him to eliminate these cover-up statements because they would ensure that his father would discount what Edward had to say. These statements masked Edward's anger at his father and at the legacy his father had given him. The final draft eliminated these "take-aways." I include Edward's entire final letter to show the difference in impact between those earlier drafts with the "take-aways" and this final letter without them.

Dear Dad,

These are some memories and feelings I want to tell you about. . . . One thing is how you treat Mom. When you have something to say to her, it usually sounds angry, very angry. I don't know what kind of response you expect, but I believe she doesn't much care for it. I don't like it at all. It infuriates me and embarrasses me. I wish I had said something about it long ago instead of keeping quiet all these years.

I remember what it was like when you were angry with me. There was no discussion, no reasoning, just fury and lashing out verbally and/or physically. I don't know which was worse. You could devastate me with either. I remember the time I was watching the kids, and you drove up. I had left the water running in the kitchen to do the dishes. I went outside to check on the girls when you drove up. When we went into the house, I saw the water running over. I was scared to death. Scared of your response. I had good reason. You beat me all the way down to the basement. The next day, you told Mike and his family what I had done, in front of me, letting them know what an unreliable, stupid kid I was. I thought you hated me and that hurt a lot. I don't think it was fair to give that kind of responsibility to an eleven year old kid. . . .

I remember feeling scared of your reaction when I was sick, too. You made me feel that I was somehow defective and that you were angry and ashamed of me. I didn't want you to know when I was sick. The time I was hospitalized and tested for migraine headaches was a nightmare. I was scared to death about what was happening to me, and scared to death that it would push you away from me forever if it was bad news. What pisses me off is that any kid deserves comfort and warmth from a parent, especially at times like that. You had nothing but impatience and disappointment to give.

The affair with Kathy is the last topic I want to tell you about. Has it ever occurred to you how embarrassing that was for me? My dad and a schoolmate. Why her, Dad? I can't believe you didn't pick her on purpose. Whether you were competing with me or just trying to hurt me, you won. The whole family paid for that one.

As far as I'm concerned, you've shown me that you are basically selfish, vengeful, and unable to display anything but anger, disappointment, and bitterness. I wish that I had said this long ago, but I realize that I was a kid and you are the one that should have known better. I want to know what you think and feel after you read this. Call or write when you are ready.

Ed

Edward sent this letter and it was taken seriously. Although his father apologized, the response to his letter was not particularly gratifying. He did not deny anything Edward wrote about, but he did try to get out of taking responsibility. Nevertheless, because Edward had finally confronted his father with what he felt and knew, he was no longer intimidated by him. It is easy to imagine what would have happened had he sent the original version: His father would not have apologized, and Edward would still be afraid, hiding his angry feelings behind niceness.

Since writing the letter exposes the writer to what he fears will happen after the letter arrives, there is a sense of exhilaration and risk taking; the letter writer finds out what it is like to express everything he wants. It is liberating for him to know that he is being clear and that whatever the response (denial, discount, abuse, distortion, acknowledgment, respect, or appreciation), he can get support. Whether the support comes from a therapist, therapy group, friends, or family, he knows that this support will help him survive the response.

By the time the writer has revised the letter, he will have examined and attempted to work through the barriers, whether psychological or linguistic, to communicating honestly. The feedback and revision process functions both to bring increased self-knowledge and to act as an antispoiler. When the final version is ready, the writer will not be spoiling his chance to communicate by alienating the reader with psychobabble or by misleading, confusing, rescuing, trivializing, or otherwise discounting himself.

PART III

Daring to Write

I was angry with my friend;
I told my wrath, my wrath did end.
I was angry with my foe:
I told it not, my wrath did grow.

—JOHN MILTON

Give sorrow words: the grief that does not speak
Whispers the o'er-fraught heart and bids it break.

—WILLIAM SHAKESPEARE

6

Butting Heads

When even requests for information can bring on attacks, it
is not surprising that letters confronting severe abuse or
severe family pathology seldom produce an open dialogue. Instead, they tend to generate a series of responses and counter-
responses that eventually help the writer to give up hope and to
understand what part of the problem is her responsibility and
what part of the problem is her parents' responsibility.

There are ways to gain control when writing a confrontational
letter. Sometimes it is helpful to write separately to each parent
to help the writer differentiate which feelings and thoughts belong to which parent. Although the writer cannot prevent her father from showing the letter meant for him to the letter writer's
mother in a way that illegitimately involves the mother, the writer
will have expressed what she wanted to express to the person to
whom she wanted to express it. If her father then chooses to pull
in his wife or passively lets her interfere, that becomes obvious.

In families in which there are covert alliances, it is often appropriate to write separately to each parent but request that both parents read both letters.

Choosing what to talk about in the first letter and what to save for a follow-up letter, and giving instructions about what the writer wants the recipient to do and not to do in response to her letter, makes the task of writing the initial letter more manageable. Giving explicit instructions to parents whom you see as too powerful is hard to do in person but fairly easy to do in a letter. An example of an instruction is: "Don't call or visit, please send me a written response; it'll be easier for me to think about what you say." Instructions can be tailored to expected responses. If, for instance, you predict from experience that the parent will do her usual "martyr trip," or blame you, or cry and ask forgiveness but not acknowledge what you say, you can ask that she not do that. You can request that she read your letter and first acknowledge what she agrees with before saying what it is she disputes.

Susanna, an anesthesiologist, could tell you the facts of her abuse, vaguely and without emotion. It took her years of therapy, including Rolfing, to get her feelings back and her body undeadened. (Rolfing is a form of body work in which connective tissue is manipulated to reorder the body by bringing the head, shoulders, thorax, pelvis, and legs into alignment.) During this time she remained in phony contact with both parents, pretending that she belonged to a close family. She cut off feelings about the family pathology, feigning normalcy. It is not uncommon for a client who comes into therapy with a masked expression to have sustained childhood abuse and to have not yet fully understood or integrated the experience.

Only when Susanna could talk about specific details of her experience could she even imagine writing her parents. Because Susanna was physically as well as emotionally abused, the idea of writing a confrontational letter home terrified her. She had to write many drafts before her letters conveyed what she really wanted to convey. In her first drafts she tried to teach her parents. Then she pleaded for understanding from a pitiful position. Finally she realized that when she wrote a single letter to both parents together, her feelings about her father blurred with her feelings about her mother. She could then avoid holding either parent responsible. She sent a few of these vague letters, but sending them gave her no relief.

Writing a separate letter to each parent clarified each parent's contribution to her mistreatment. During the writing process she became increasingly aware of how long she had protected her parents, letting them off the hook for their persistent physical and emotional abuse.

1. Dear Mr. Kagan,

I want you to feel the terror and pain that you inflicted on me as a child. You were a bastard, a madman, a tyrant. . . . It was like living with a monster—you could be teaching us about the sun and the moon one minute and a half-hour later you'd be beating me. . . . This is what you did:

I was in the first grade. We were having supper. I was on your left, the girls to your right, and Mom jumping up and down to get the food. You "caught me" biting my nails. You slapped my hands and yelled that I am not to do that and that you will get me to stop by painting them with gentian violet— that your intention is to shame me by making sure everyone sees the deep purple on my nails and that the bad taste will get me to quit. You got up and headed to the bathroom to get the gentian violet. . . . You returned, a scowl on your face, gruffly told me to give you my hands—I begged you not to do it, and you grabbed them. . . . Mom asking you if you have to do it and

*your responding, "It's the only way she'll learn." . . . I walked
to school slowly the next day so I could scrape it off before I got
to Miss White's room. When dinner time rolled around the next
evening, you told me to take my hands out. I refused. You yanked
them out from behind my back, dragged me down the hall . . .
belted me in my bedroom, and took me into the bathroom to
paint them again. I was mortified. Every day I went to school I
kept my hands in my pockets or balled up my hands in a fist. . . .
Why do you think I was biting my nails in the first place—you
terrorized me from the time I was little, and anxious kids bite
their nails. If shaming had been your goal, it worked. But if
your intent was to get me to stop biting my nails, it didn't.*

*About the same time (age six) you criticized my weight. "Oh
Jesus cohany—stop eating so much, you can't have another
helping" and you YELLED for me to PUT IT DOWN. I was
not to get another helping because I was ALREADY TOO
FAT. You ordered me to get up from the table and run around
the block SIX TIMES to burn off some of the fat. Mom, in her
whiny pleading tone, stated, "Frank, she's only six years old."
Your reply, "I don't care, she needs to exercise." You leaned
over my chair, pointed to the door, and yelled "GET GOING,
NOW!!! and don't come back until you've done all six
blocks." . . . I hung my head to hide the tears. I got questions
from the neighbors (it's hard to miss a six year old making repeated trips around the block). I covered up for you . . . I was
ashamed to tell them the truth, that you were crazy and that
you scared me and made me feel like dirt. Meanwhile outside
of our house you presented yourself as a model father and always giving to the community. . . .*

*. . . I was still wetting the bed as a seven/eight year old. I'd
come into your room to tell Mom that I had wet the bed and
that I needed help changing the sheets—I'd be crying because*

there was nothing I could do to keep from wetting the bed. You called me a big baby, yelled at me, and said that I was too old for this and that I should just sleep in it. Why do you think I was wetting the bed? No place was safe in our house, least of all my bed. It was a place of torture, pain, and invasion. Mom used my bed as her examining table to check my head for lice, my ears for wax, and my anus for worms. My bedroom was where you'd drag me in order to beat me. You'd grab whatever arm you could, yanking it hard enough that my arm felt like it would come out of my shoulder, then jerking my hands behind my back and holding them with one hand while you undid your belt and jerked it out of your pants (to this day my elbows and shoulders bother me) . . . you forced my head into my bed to muffle the sound and decrease my struggling, while you yanked my pants down and t-shirt up to belt my bare skin. You strapped me over and over again, while I screamed for you to stop. . . . The sting and welts on my back, buttocks, and legs lasted for hours—I couldn't sit down.

I seem to remember you saying that if I didn't struggle then you wouldn't be forced to hit anything but my buttocks. What did you expect me to do but fight to get away—you were so out of control, so much of a madman over something as little as my not coming the first time you called or "for talking back." I learned that if I breathed shallowly and went limp and into a trance when you were beating me I could get away from the pain and fear and most of all YOU. You took things one step further. You contaminated tender touch with physical abuse. After beating me, you'd turn me over, sit me up and try to hug me, and stroke my hair or cheek. HOW FRAUDULENT!! You tried to get close to me after just beating me. I survived your abuse only by dropping reality and going into my own world. I became rigid and looked at the floor when you touched me tenderly. You'd tell me you "didn't like to have to do this, that you wouldn't have to if I would just listen" as if to say I MADE YOU BEAT ME!!

I've moved from feeling suffocated by you, so much so that the only clean air and safe place was under my bed or when I could walk outside of the house—to being strangled by my rage, wanting to throw up, regurgitate you from my system— to wanting to strangle you for the emotional, physical, and financial costs I've suffered as a result of your abuse.

I can hear you now—was it that bad? Didn't you have some joy as a child, didn't I provide you with what you needed? Yes, you gave me material things. . . . But this didn't begin to touch the time, happiness, and money I've lost as a result of your abuse. I've spent endless amounts of time alone or in bad relationships, depressed and anxious. It's only through therapy and hard work that I've been repairing the damage you inflicted on me. You robbed me of the pleasure of my own body—my ability to feel graceful, to enjoy sports, you stole the pleasure of the touch of a man who loves me—you gave me a barren and effortful existence.

You have shown me in all of your responses to my letters that you are incapable of acknowledging . . . (e.g., "the abuse just happened," "I swore I would never do it to my kids," and in your most recent letter—"I abused all of you"). Hence, I am now seeking payment for the resulting damage, the cost of my therapies (all of it to date and expected in the future). I've had to forgo simple pleasures (e.g., a weekend away, a nice dinner out, a new piece of clothing) because of the hundreds of dollars I've had to spend. . . .

As you know, the episodes I described here are just a few early examples . . . you continued abusing me until I left for college.

Attached are the bills for my recent and past therapies, diagnostic procedures and surgeries, and projected therapy expenses. . . .

Susanna

Unlike her earlier vague letters (which I have not reprinted), this letter made an impact. But although he acknowledged that he had abused Susanna, her father quickly shifted to a defensive victim stance. He told her that his violent father had made his childhood miserable. He claimed that Susanna's letter surprised him because he was unaware of how he had re-created the abuse. His stance as passive bystander as well as his shift in focus away from her to his own father's abuse of him distressed Susanna. But finally telling her father what was in her mind and heart left her feeling good about herself, in spite of her father's ultimately defensive response.

Often the victim of abuse cannot accept that both parents are in some way participating. Not until the writer confronts one parent successfully does she become strong enough to acknowledge that the other parent is colluding in the behavior. A clear letter to one parent works to dislodge old protective stances toward the other parent. Getting clear about her father's contribution to her unhappy childhood uncorked Susanna's feelings about the active role her mother played in her misery. For the first time Susanna held her mother responsible not only for failing to protect her children but also for abusing them herself. The letter Susanna wrote was in stark contrast to any previous communication with her mother:

2. *Dear Mom,*
   This letter is long overdue—I realized that I need to tell you how I feel about the ways you treated me as a kid and the way

*you interact with me as an adult. . . . When we were growing
up you were too busy using us to fill your gaps/inadequacies—
kids were born into our family to serve three functions: as
cleaning and food preparation services, as parents and protec-
tors, and to bring honor to the Kagan name.*

*First, we were cheap labor . . . housecleaning, lawn mow-
ing, laundry, washing and waxing boat and/or cars, cleaning
garage and laundry room, changing beds, canning food, etc.
etc. etc. (some of which went late into the night).*

*You couldn't have operated that household without us, and
for the longest time, even after we were gone (almost every visit
home entailed helping you sew, catch up on your housekeep-
ing, etc.). I distinctly remember being yanked out of bed early
every Saturday morning to face a list of things Dad expected us
to have done on his arrival home, and your getting to go off to
grocery shop and have your hair done.*

*I resented your being able to escape while we stayed home
to do the housework (remember we had worked all week at
school, and doing homework after school with little or no
chance to watch TV or play), but far worse was your neglect of
your maternal duty—TO KEEP YOUR CHILDREN SAFE.*

*You left us with a madman and . . . you chose REPEAT-
EDLY TO LOOK THE OTHER WAY. When we were home
on a holiday, you sounded shocked regarding Musia getting
beaten with the oar from the Sunfish as if you had no idea that
it had occurred . . . there was NO WAY you could have missed
the bruises and abrasions on her body. . . . Furthermore, you
offered NO COMFORT to any of us around any of the
abuse—instead you kept enabling it to happen over and over.*

*If you happened to be home when Dad was punishing us,
you did nothing or in your teary, whimper voice, "you don't
have to do it so hard," as if to say hitting was OK just not . . .*

so hard or in ways that the neighbors might find out. I at least
had the guts to fight it (trying to sit down as I got dragged down
the hall) or actively interceding on the girls' behalf, physically
getting between Dad and Musia in order to get him to stop
beating the daylights out of her. I took all the risks—I was out
on a limb with no one there for me.

. . . I still picture us sitting at the breakfast table before
Church one Sunday. Musia and Hannah had begun doing
something that Dad was escalating into something major
without having been present when it occurred. I could see that
they were going to get smacked or belted if no one intervened
so I accused him of having no right to jump to conclusions
when he wasn't even there. All the while you were kicking me
under the table and glaring at me as if I was doing something
wrong. . . . Dad hauled off and slapped me across the face so
hard I had his hand-print on my face for hours afterward and
can still feel it to this day. . . . All you could say was, "LOOK
AT HER—HOW CAN WE GO TO CHURCH—WHAT
WILL THE NEIGHBORS SAY WHEN THEY SEE HER!!"
Your words stung worse than my face. I didn't care what the
neighbors said—fuck the God-damned neighbors and fuck
you for your insensitivity . . . all you cared about were the
God-damned family secrets, someone might find out that the
Kagan prestige and happy home was a veneer and rotten
underneath.

. . . The pressure to perform, be efficient, "make maximum"
use of our time was endless. . . . God forbid you just sit and
watch TV (as Dad often did), you should be doing something
(such as sewing, repair, baking, picking up the basement).
Quiet time, reading, or single activities were not accepted—
there was always something that had to be done first. And yet,
all that frenetic activity, lists of things to do, all that chaos, did

not result in anything ever being finished—it just made for anxious, driven, hyper vigilant kids (to not be so resulted in more abuse and criticism). We lived in a pressure cooker.

One of many Saturdays Julie had called to ask me to go shopping with her, taking the bus (which cost all of 25 cents each way). For once, you went to bat for us with Dad . . . I was INCREDIBLY THANKFUL that we were getting to do something fun and wanted to get you something to show you my appreciation. I spent the whole time I was shopping with Julie trying to find something—it couldn't be seen as too expensive, wasteful, frivolous, etc. Try finding something for under $2.00 that meets all those . . . a florist had a dozen sweetheart roses for $1.99. Picked up a little card and wrote down thanks for letting us spend the day out. Walked up from the bus stop so I wouldn't waste a dime calling you to come get me and excitedly gave you the flowers. All you could say was "What did you go and do that for? How much did they cost? I wish you hadn't gotten them because they're gonna die. . . ."

. . . You always expected us to do perfectly in school. . . . Whenever I would get a grade in the low 90's or high 80's (and I'm not talking for the ten week period—I'm saying for that one test), I would immediately run to Mr. Mason and get him to let me drop the class because I was terrified to bring home anything but perfection. The cost of that style of coping was great. I missed out on accelerated classes and teachers who encouraged independent thinking all because of the God-damned grade and the fear of showing you a grade. Learning was a chore, a terrifying situation, not a challenge or a joy. . . .

. . . You could never tune into what I was feeling or needing. . . . I drove back from New Hampshire in a blinding snowstorm after going from NC to NH in one day and going through my divorce. The first thing out of your mouth as I arrived home was "Don't you think that you just made the biggest mistake of your life?" NOPE, my biggest mistake was coming home.

. . . you were always competing with me—I would come home excited about having done something I was proud of and you'd shit on it. The Benson Scholar award is a prime example. I was one of 200 undergrads nominated for this scholarship and service award and one of ten who finally got it. I was thrilled, and all you could say was "How much money did you get?" . . .

You once said you felt that having your kids get divorced made you feel you failed as a mother—well you did—you failed to keep us safe, to understand how I felt while I was growing up and now, and failed to recognize what I needed. I get furious with your continued wistfulness when you talk about Gary. I was suicidal during our marriage—Gary and I needed the divorce—it was just like living at home again. . . .

Now, having said all of this, this is how I predict you all will react. Mom, I expect you to cry a lot . . . saying things like "Oh, if I could just go back and redo things," I expect you to talk to the girls and get their support that you "weren't such a bad mother" . . . and you will still never address it with me directly. I expect Dad to reassure you that you did the best that you could. I can also see any and all of you saying, "poor Susanna, she always has to go back and look at things that are old history and don't matter now." I would be happy if these predictions were wrong.

. . . it's amazing I turned out as well as I have—I have myself and my therapy group to thank.

Susanna

Susanna was used to getting beaten or strongly criticized when she was honest, so her mother's response letter admitting that she had not protected her children from her husband's abusive behavior was a surprise. Delighted, Susanna wrote back a grateful letter:

3. *Dear Mom,*

Your Christmas letter meant a lot to me. It was the most personal letter you've ever written to me . . . you reread my letters, "listened to" the specific events I discussed, but most important acknowledged my feelings. . . . You also owned up to your part in the abuse—your indifference, lack of empathy, abandonment, leaving me to fend for myself, and your avoidance of taking a firm stand against Dad. I feel really good about this as a beginning of mending our relationship. . . .

Love,
Susanna

Susanna expected that her mother's good letter and her appreciative response would open the way to an improved relationship. She was bitterly disappointed when her mother reverted to defensive put-downs in her next letter. Susanna's fourth letter reflects this disappointment. It also illustrates how tenuous the tendrils of goodwill can be at this point in the communication process.

4. *Dear Mom,*

You never cease to amaze me. Without missing a beat, you try to tell me about your latest guru lecturer's views on therapy and recovery; after all "he is a psychologist." My god, Mom, what am I—chopped liver? You continue to ignore my feelings just like when we were growing up and turn to a complete

stranger *for advice. I'll be the judge on when I am finished
with therapy, not you or anyone else.*

*. . . I thought your indifference toward Dad's abuse was bad
enough, but if you are telling the truth about this and did
secretly tell people about Dad's abuse of us while telling us
to keep quiet about it, you've outdone yourself—how dare
you! . . . For years I made excuses for you—"poor Mom, Dad is
so critical of her, no one to support her, she works so hard, he
wants to keep her under his thumb, we had to advocate for her,
protect her." Man was I off. You had the support of friends. . . .
You have a lot of nerve negotiating the bill. . . . The bill is not
negotiable. You're getting off cheap as far as I'm concerned. . . .*
                                                        Susanna

The letter exchange helped Susanna understand that her parents were capable, when pressed, of only limited acknowledgment,
followed by defensiveness or promises, followed by retractions.
In a phone conversation, her father promised to pay her past, present, and future treatment expenses. Then, in a letter following
this conversation, he said he needed the money for travel (he was
off to Norway with her mother) and to support her mother if she
should get sick. At around this same time, Susanna received a letter from her parent's lawyer suggesting that the statute of limita-
tions was up and Susanna would have no legal recourse for
obtaining money from her parents related to their abuse of her.

In the past this approach, a little acknowledgment and ap-
peasement and then retraction and bullying, had always worked.
Her parents could then go on ignoring Susanna. In letter number
one to her father, Susanna discusses how he used to beat her
when she asserted herself and then behave affectionately when
she cried. Susanna came to recognize that her father continually
repeated this same cycle: abuse followed by affection, or affec-

tion followed by betrayal. But this time Susanna was confident. She consulted her lawyer. Her lawyer wrote her father to request his tax records.

Susanna continued to request reimbursement for treatment expenses. Her parents knew she was willing to sue. They finally sent her money to cover her past treatment bills. The letter her father sent with the payment fully acknowledged his responsibility in the abuse. The butting of heads ceased. With the confrontation of both of her parents behind her, Susanna has accomplished what she set out to accomplish. She is aware of her angry feelings as well as her positive feelings; these include pleasure in her own body and in her achievements. She rarely sets herself up to be mistreated by landlords, bosses, or friends. She has a harder time dealing with romantic relationships; she has misjudged men she feels attracted to and still has difficulty standing up for herself if a man she likes becomes hostile and defensive. She is painfully aware of this and very motivated to change her pattern with men, as she changed her pattern with her parents.

Her "butting heads" series of letters home resulted in a loss of hope about her parents' ability to acknowledge her or to be close to her unless she continually made efforts to confront them. Even when she was constantly vigilant and confrontational, this would produce only a brief period of honesty and closeness. Susanna's letters provided an important reality check for her. Although Susanna had not repressed or forgotten the abuse, she had denied how bad it was, denied her mother's part in it, and denied her rage and sadness. For a person like Susanna, who has grown up in a family where reality is given short shrift, the reality test is a long-overdue validation of feelings and perceptions.

Response letters provide evidence of reality, and they do not depend on an outside witness such as a therapist. With letters, one can witness for oneself.

Susanna recently attended her niece's confirmation with her entire family. For the last few years she had avoided family gatherings because she would revert to her old way of distancing herself from her feelings by working hard to take care of the rest of the family. After these family visits she would become anxious, disorganized, panicky, and emotionally labile. It usually took her a week or two to recover fully. But during this last visit she avoided pseudo-discussions with her parents. She spent time only with the family members she liked. She had fun. She knew she had broken out of her rigid role.

Her years of group therapy have been very effective, but the most pivotal work she has done, with the help of her group, has been the confrontation of her past and of her parents in her letters.

7

The Role of Other Family Members

HELPING OR HINDERING

Families, like individuals, can get mired in an unhealthy pattern. Each family member may play a part in keeping the pattern stable and static. This gives each member the potential to powerfully affect the family system and to affect the family member who dares to challenge that system, either as an ally or an adversary.

A family member who is proud of the writer for confronting the parent can be invaluable in supporting the letter writer. When this happens, even if the parent is very defensive, change within the family system can be rapid. When the family is highly dysfunctional, an up-front letter supported by one or more family members may not change the family pattern, but it can set a healthy precedent.

When the son or daughter confronts one parent—for example, the mother (as Dave does in Chapter 14)—the father may be forced to make a decision. The easiest decision, if the mother is enraged and demanding his allegiance, is to support her. After all, he is living with her and the writer is out of the home. He has to deal daily with the repercussions of the letter. Supporting the content of the letter is tantamount to confronting his wife, a step he may never have taken or may have taken with little or no success. Most likely he does not have the backing of therapy or the allies that the letter writer has. So the writer's father (even if he agrees with the letter writer) may not be willing or able to follow the writer's lead and thus may not be able to risk changing the old system. Being aware of these strong pulls toward stasis between the parents will help reduce the writer's sense of surprise or betrayal when, for example, his father does not stand firmly behind him. The letter writer needs to entertain the strong possibility that his confrontation of one family member will change his relationship to everyone in the family.

Siblings, like the "other" parent, can be supportive of the writer's efforts or can undermine those efforts. A sister may be sympathetic to the writer's issues with his parents because she may have the same or similar issues. The writer's confrontation may make it easier for the sister to do her own confronting. Or a sister may have already confronted the parent and may welcome the writer as an ally. If the parents are closed to what the writer has to say, they are likely to go to their other children for validation and support. If even one sibling out of many supports the writer's efforts, it can have a powerful impact on parents and therefore on the whole family system.

The writer's brother, for example, may tell the parents that he is surprised and dismayed by how angry and defensive they are. He can do this even if he does not have the same issues with his parents that the writer does. Knowing ahead of time that you have the support of one brother or sister or aunt or uncle makes sending the letter less frightening. It helps to plan ahead by enlisting whatever support may be available from other family members. Although occasionally the surprise factor helps shake up the family system, it is generally useful to avoid surprises. Tell your sisters and brothers that you are writing a letter to your parents confronting issues you have with them. If you trust your sister or brother and want to become closer to them, tell them your goals, your hopes, and your fears. When you have prepared in this way, copies sent to these family members will keep everything aboveboard.

As many clients have discovered the hard way, it is important that the writer not try to get his siblings or other family members to admit to feeling or thinking the same way he does about his parents. The sibling has often had different experiences with the parent and so has a different perspective. Even if his sister feels or thinks the same way as the letter writer, she may not be ready to admit it. Any attempt by the letter writer to require his sister to mirror him instead of merely support him can backfire.

Siblings are often unaware, afraid, or in denial of the issues the writer intends to bring up with his parents. They may not want the writer to rock the boat. They may work hard at keeping the old, familiar, unhealthy pattern of the family intact. This can translate into reassuring the parents that they are fine parents and that they should not pay any attention to a mean-spirited and ungrateful letter. A sibling may see the letter home as an opportunity to step ahead of the writer in a longstanding competition. It helps to remember that the family pattern is a type of pseudo-solution to a problem, and just because the writer may be ready to give up the old pattern and pseudo-solution does not mean others are.

It is easy to discern whether siblings will be supportive. Often the writer's revealed plans elicit strong reactions from brothers and sisters. If a sibling tries to dissuade the writer from sending a letter, that sibling is unlikely to support the writer. The writer can then ask that this sibling at least not interfere.

One word of caution: Twice in my experience, a client who had not checked out whether her brothers and sisters were supportive erred by revealing the contents of her letter to them before she sent it to her parents. Because they were threatened by the letter's challenge to the status quo, the siblings tried to confiscate the letter before the parents got it. If the writer is not sure how the other family members will take her letter, it is better to put notes to siblings in a cover letter with a copy of the letter that has already been sent to the parents. This careful timing prevents the other family members from undermining the process before the parents have had a chance to read the letter.

Ken, whose letters home appear in Chapter 9, tried to get each of his siblings to support him in his efforts to break down barriers in the family. He was unsuccessful. His brothers and his sister advised him not to confront his parents and to make his peace with them. When Ken sent his letter to his parents, he sent an individual cover letter to each of his siblings. The one to Carl is typical:

Dear Carl,

. . . I've enclosed a copy of a note I sent to Mom and Dad after our most recent telephone conversation. I've sent a copy to Georgia and James, too. I would like to talk with you about my original letter to Mom and Dad. I would not be surprised if you have some of the same issues I have and some that I don't. Even if you don't want to talk about it, I'd like you to acknowledge that you received it. I'd also like to know how it made you feel about me, us, and the family.

Hope to hear from you soon.

Ken

After a number of written exchanges with his parents, characterized by defensive denials and blaming, and with his brothers
and his sister, characterized by their pleas that he bury his anger
and let the past stay in the past, Ken gave up hope of being
known and cared for by his family. He felt as if he had lost his
parents, and he felt alienated and unsupported by his siblings.
He wrote a final letter reflecting these feelings (see Chapter 17).

Ken then broke off contact with his siblings for about two
years. When one brother and his sister had crises in their lives,
which involved the parents, they called Ken, told him he was
right about their parents, and said that they had many of the
same feelings that Ken had expressed in his letters home. However, they did not apologize for failing to support him earlier.
Their belated responses were perfunctory, failing to generate any
intimacy.

Four years after Ken's final letter, his brother Carl, whom he
had not heard from, wrote him an extraordinary letter. It contained a genuine apology. Carl explained that it had taken him all
this time to understand that Ken's view of the destructive way the
family interacted was accurate. He talked about what his life had
been like and how Ken's letter had inspired him to go into therapy. Carl's letter was warm and generous and open. Carl invited
Ken to write back, and Ken (who had given up on ever being intimate with anyone in his family) and Carl are involved in an increasingly intimate letter exchange.

It is often realistic for the writer to fear that his whole family
will rally against him. Many of the letter writers in this book went
ahead with no support from family members. Sometimes the
family did rally against them, but the writers were prepared. Even
in these cases, the letters disrupted their families' rigid pattern,
often irrevocably changing the family. Sometimes a family re-

configures in a much healthier way long after the letter arrives, and sometimes a family member will surprise the writer by belatedly becoming an ally, as Carl did with Ken. Especially when the letter exposes and confronts abuse and/or secrets, the letter forces at least some change in each family member, even when the rest of the family is in lockstep to maintain the status quo. And this change generally affects future generations.

Ideally the letter writer is willing to lose those siblings or parents with whom she has had relationships based on illusion and family pathology. It helps if she is sending the letter primarily for herself and not in hopes of rescuing the family, the other parent, her sisters, or her brothers. It is best if the writer first speaks up for herself and then speaks up for others.

However, crises involving another family member can sometimes embolden the writer to articulate and assert complex feelings to a parent that she has never had the courage to express. Often the writer, so inspired, attempts to rescue another family member when she has not yet saved herself. This can work when the rescue attempt functions as a trial run for the writer before she feels strong enough to confront on her own behalf. After this initial trial run, she is often able to be open about how she feels the parent has treated her.

The motivation to rescue her father was the starting point for Nora. In the past she had had a terrible time acknowledging her anger and her criticisms of her mother or anybody else. She was dishonest with her feelings, often acting sweet but being mean and competitive in sneaky ways. When her father was rendered helpless with Alzheimer's disease and became utterly dependent on his wife, Nora strongly identified with him. Spurred on by rage at her mother for putting her father's life in jeopardy, Nora is for the first time openly critical of her mother:

Dear Mom,

I have had many thoughts and feelings about our recent weekend get-together, most of them upsetting.

I am especially concerned with Dad and his having Alzheimer's. He is very vulnerable. When I thought of him going with you to the airport and sitting in the car while you went inside, I knew that there was no telling how long you would be, if Dierdre's plane was late, her luggage delayed, you missed her in the airport, etc. What were you thinking leaving Dad? What if the police had come up and told him he had to move the car? Between his double vision and the Alzheimer's, there is no way he should have been exposed to such a possibility both in terms of endangering himself and others. O'Hare is such an incredibly confusing place. I'm sure he was upset just thinking about it.

When you left for the airport, you left very late, which assured you would have to speed. In doing that you endanger you, Dad, and others on the road. Then I understand that coming back from the airport you were again driving too fast, endangering everyone, Dierdre too, and Dad complained so many times that you pulled over and had him sit in the back. The problem is not Dad's worrying, but your bad reckless driving . . . at age seventy-nine your reaction time is bad and so your driving is even worse.

Driving home from the airport, you got lost. I couldn't believe that when you pulled over in a very dangerous neighborhood, you sent Dad in for directions. Had you forgotten that Dad has Alzheimer's? I heard that he was so upset that afterwards he started getting into the wrong car and didn't even recognize his own car of many years. . . . I'm sure he was very scared and very upset.

The next day returning from the beach I was upset to find you in the dining room poring through the PDR. I thought to myself, "What is she doing?" Dierdre thought you were looking up a prescription that another doctor had written. I was more suspicious. I looked in your medicine cabinets and found medicines that you had written prescriptions for, for Dad. It is totally inappropriate and unethical for you to still be writing prescriptions. Dad was not in an emergency and if he was it is only appropriate to call his doctors. That's what they are there for.

You stopped practicing medicine at least twenty years ago. You locate the best doctors in Chicago for Dad and then you undercut their ability to help Dad by still acting like you're his doctor. I will call Dad's doctor to make sure he is aware that you are still doing this and see what advice I can get as to how to get you to stop. Even you told me before that he was upset when you were messing with Dad's heart medicine. Did the doctors know that you upped Dad's tranquilizer the night before he went into surgery? If I had my way, for your sake and Dad's, I would have your prescription pad taken away. Are you so out of it that you don't understand how wrong and bad what you are doing is?

I also understand that the day Dad was to go for his spinal tap you had him out in the heat during a health advisory doing manual work in the yard. . . . Your terrible judgment endangers him. It reminds me of the time a few years ago when you went in the ocean at Compo Beach after a tropical storm. The waves were very high. It was very dangerous. Mostly only the life guards were in the water. You went in and then Dad went in after you in fear for you. I was so angry when I saw John and Russell have to go in the surf to pull both of you out.

Dad has told me that you have expressed suicidal thoughts and your behavior supports that. If you want to die, that is a decision only you can make, but taking Dad with you is not right.

Before the weekend was over you shared with me your latest trip idea that you and Dad go on a bicycle trip to Holland. That is crazy. In my memory you and Dad have never ridden a bike. . . . There is no way he should make a trip like that, and given your lack of biking experience, you shouldn't either. . . . This is truly a bad idea that unfortunately Dad feels powerless to back out of no matter how much he doesn't want to go.

I write this letter in hope that you will get help for your sake and Dad's, but I doubt it because I expect that you will deny that any of this is a problem.

Nora

Nora sent copies of this letter to her brothers and sisters and to her father's doctor. Her mother never acknowledged reading the letter, but she slightly toned down her behavior. Although the impact on her mother was minimal, the impact on Nora was startling. She is no longer compelled to work for her mother's approval or to deny her feelings of dislike and anger. Nora's letter was the beginning of finding her own voice. She is increasingly able to express what she is really feeling instead of pretending to feel one thing and acting out another. She would not have confronted her mother on her own behalf, but writing on her father's behalf gave her the jump start she needed to continue to be forthright.

....

Stan also had a hard time being honest with anyone—especially women, and especially his mother. He had been in two bad marriages with women who, like his mother, couldn't be trusted. He had married them not because he wanted to but because they wanted to and he did not want them to be mad at him. Like Nora, Stan was not willing to confront his mother on his own behalf, but seeing his nieces (his sister Rhonda's daughters) being abused and his mother's role in their abuse forced him to confront his mother. Stan understood that he was really writing for himself as well and that he needed the extra motivation of helping his nieces to get him over his fear and resistance. Stan stood up for his nieces and supported his sister Jane, who was caring for them, against the efforts of his mother and Rhonda. (Rhonda had initially run away from her husband, Vince, because he was abusing her and the children, but she quickly decided to go back to him and tried to get her children to come with her. She was enraged when Jane and Stan supported the children staying where it would be safe.) Stan did for his nieces what he had not been able to do for himself.

Dear Mom:

You should know by now that information travels quickly, so I heard of your conversation with Jane. I wish I could say that I cannot believe the things you said to her, but unfortunately I can believe them.

I am angry that after all everyone has been through, you are supporting Rhonda's delusions and helping her stay with Vince rather than helping her save herself and the children. Your daughter is in deep trouble; you are aware that this man has seriously injured her many times before, has threatened to kill her, and will eventually succeed. Her daughters have been through hell, and all signs point to their being physically and sexually abused. You have plenty of evidence that Rhonda is a deeply troubled person who at this point has no capacity to make good decisions and take care of herself or the kids. Rather than stepping in as her mother and trying to push her

*in the direction of getting help, of getting safety, you refuse to
get involved by pretending that Rhonda is indeed OK and safe
with Vince. That puts your daughter in danger of being further
abused, beaten, and losing her life.*

*As I told you, I was angry that you would blame me for go-
ing "outside the family" to involve the Department of Social
Services in a last, desperate attempt to save those children and
perhaps to save Rhonda as well. While I hated to have to do
that, there was no way I could sit on the information about
abuse of the kids. It was clear by then that nothing else had
any chance of working. I was stunned and angry that when
Rhonda was hiding from Vince at Jane's house, where you sent
her so he wouldn't find her at your house, you made her call
Vince to tell him to stop calling you. You asked Rhonda to call
the man she was hiding from, because he tried to kill her, so
that you wouldn't have to tell him yourself to stop calling you.
You should not have done that when you know Rhonda's ability to stay away from him is nonexistent anyway.*

*I am angry at your willingness to pretend there isn't a prob-
lem to avoid having to deal with the situation. You have seen
graphic evidence yourself of how brutally Rhonda has been
treated; and you have graphic evidence from her desperate
phone calls and appearances at your door that my sister, your
daughter, is sick, unable to care either for herself or the kids.
Rhonda completed two pages in her own handwriting that she
filed with the court last week, seeking protection from Vince,
documenting the physical abuse by him and stating her own
suspicions that her daughters have been abused, and her guilt
keeps forcing her back to be abused herself. I couldn't live with
my own guilt if I stood by and let these things continue to happen. And Mom, you should think about how you will feel if*

Rhonda and the kids are further abused and you didn't try your best to end that situation.

All this has been extremely difficult, extremely wearing, and at the cost of knowing Rhonda would hate us, not love us, for doing what had to be done. I expected that; I didn't expect you would end up denouncing us as well.

I know you're shocked to hear this, since straight talk has not been the style in this family. But I am unwilling to sit on this because I am furious at how you are treating me, treating Rhonda, the children, and my other sisters, especially Jane.

The case worker from social services is likely to call you to ask what you know about the situation. For the sake of Rhonda and her children, I hope you tell them candidly what you know has happened to her in the past. Rhonda and the kids need you now more than ever. Also, you should tell Dad the truth. He'll find out eventually anyway. And now it leaves him thinking we grossly overreacted since the only problem is that Rhonda's husband occasionally loses his temper, when the truth is that he is a dangerous man.

Stan

Confronting the family secrets and the family pathology helped Stan to get disentangled from his mother, and that helped him to end the relationship with his second wife. Stan's original letter, like Nora's, was motivated by rescue, but it enabled him to go beyond rescue. When Stan wrote this letter he had already separated from his wife, but his wife was furious that he had left her. He appeased her by agreeing to do things with her when he did not really want to be with her. In this way he kindled her hopes that they would reunite. He felt dependent on her for her agreement that the marriage should end and she would not give it. He was angry at her and ashamed of himself for still wanting her approval. This was bad for both of them. After writing his mother, he wrote his wife, ending the unhealthy connection they had maintained.

Although some use rescue of other family members to propel them to confront parents on their own behalf, others need to resolve conflicts with siblings before they can resolve conflicts with parents. Allen's letter home came long after his younger sister, Jenny, had confronted the sick family dynamics and been labeled crazy by Allen and all the other members of the family.

Not only had Allen not been her ally because he was jealous of the attention his mother gave Jenny, he had actively undermined Jenny's efforts to be honest with their parents. Even with this history, when he could admit the extent to which he had undermined Jenny and tell her why he behaved in this way, he could repair their relationship. Now Jenny is, for the most part, an ally in his efforts to deal with his parents, and he is finally an ally to her. I include both Allen's letter to Jenny and a few of his letters to his parents that deal with the sibling relationships in the family:

> *Dear Jen,*
>
> *I have read your letter many times. . . . I know how scary writing to me must be, since I have always responded so poorly to you in the past. It's time for me to try to do it differently; I hope this letter will begin to close some of the distance that lies between us.*
>
> *Let me begin by confessing that I have been unfairly angry at you ever since I can remember. When you were a baby I was angry at you for getting so much attention from Mom. Mom made it real clear that she kept having babies until she got a girl, and I think she treated you special because you were a girl. My memory growing up was that you always got your way*

if we had a dispute. Now in hindsight I can see that my anger was misdirected; the problem began with Mom and you were a convenient target. When I think back I can't remember ever playing with you. I can't really believe that possible but I don't remember. I think what it means is that I wasn't much of a big brother to you; I was so busy being angry that I neglected you, lost out from really getting to know you.

Sometime around when I was in Junior High School I re-member this idea got started in our family that Dad and I were the achievers in our family, but we were basically stupid and did well only because we worked so hard. You and Mom and Saul were supposed to be the really smart ones but lacked our plodding discipline. I felt hurt having my efforts dismissed like this, and even though I knew Mom was the source for this put-down, I got mad at you, the messenger. I didn't want to believe that Mom could think of me like that. It was much easier for me to be angry at you. . . .

I stayed angry at you when you were in college and became involved in the women's movement. I experienced this as a battle between the women in the house versus the men in the house. I remember many times when you and Mom would be espousing some feminist position and I felt that if I disagreed I was a bad person. I felt my maleness was threatened. Dad, who always acts so guilty about not doing more housework, was a terrible ally for me because he wouldn't defend himself. Some-how, I would end up mostly angry at you even though a lot of what it all was about, I think, was Mom having an indirect way to express her anger and resentment of Dad. Looking back, I can see how unjust it was for me to be angry at you and also how chickenshit and self-serving. I could snipe back at Mom by attacking you, but not lose my privileged position, which I would have lost if I directly confronted Mom. The bot-

tom line, I think, is that we were both pawns in the war be-
tween Mom and Dad.

In your letter you write that I have more power than I know
within the family. You are right, as the eldest child and being
aligned with Dad has given me privileges that neither you nor
Saul ever had. . . . I have been angry at you for all the atten-
tion you got from Mom, ignoring how much this attention was
actually hurting you, and how much attention I was getting
from Dad.

When you were breaking away from Mom and Dad toward
the end of college, I was really shitty to you. Instead of sup-
porting your emotional growth as a good brother would have
done, I insisted on keeping you in the role of the little sister,
but even worse—I betrayed you and scapegoated you as the
"crazy one in the family."

. . . I am very sorry for the damage I have done to you.

Allen

Dear Dad,

When we last talked you said the only way you could think
of to "fix" things between me and Mom was not to talk for a
while and hope things got better by themselves.

I got off the phone then without giving you some informa-
tion you should have:

1. I don't want you to "fix" things between Mom and me. I
would prefer to have separate relationships with each of you
and don't like it when you get in the middle.

2. Mom stayed on the phone with me as long as I was being
indirect. When I told her I was uncomfortable with her taking
my daughter to Europe this year, she pressed me about next year.
When I told her I was uncomfortable with her taking Myra to

Europe without my son because it brought up all the messed up gender relationships in my own childhood, she got off the phone abruptly. How can Mom and I work anything out if she won't even allow me to state my criticisms or express my anger?

3. What I was referring to specifically is that Mom acted as if she deeply resented raising Saul and me for as long as I can remember. Mom always sided with Jen in every argument, routinely criticized all the men in the family because they were men, and showered Jen with gifts that Saul and I never got.

4. Since my kids were born, Mom has repeated this pattern with Lyle and Myra, always showing far more interest in her than him. I used to think the reason for this was because Mom didn't like infants. But the pattern has persisted since then even though Lyle is quite independent—and I can only conclude that it has to do with the fact he is a boy and she is a girl.

5. The gender problems in our family have clearly been confusing to Jen, Saul, and me, and it is the issue all of us are having to straighten out now that we are adults.

6. I agree with you that little would be gained by rehashing all the problems of the past. However, there needs to be a way for me to protect my own kids from these problems in our family, and the only way I can think of to do it is to tell you when I am uncomfortable with something you are proposing to do or an interaction you had with my kids.

I hope that Mom is able to understand the difference between my criticisms of some of her behaviors and disliking her. I hope that you are willing to maintain a relationship with me even if I have some criticisms of the way gender relations were and are handled in our family.

Love,
Allen

Dear Mom,

I was glad things worked out so well when I visited, but I didn't take care of myself in the museum gift shop and I want to set it right now. As I have mentioned to you on several occasions, I have noticed that you always spend much more money on Myra than Lyle, and it has become so noticeable that it makes him feel bad and it makes me feel angry. For me it brings up all the favoritism you showed me . . . [compared to] Saul, during the years when you and he were having a rough time. (The shoe is now on the other foot apparently, because he gets boxes of silver and I get broken steak knives.)

I was glad that I pointed out to you that Lyle is the person in our family who does most of the drawing and that he should also get one of the fancy drawing pencils you got Myra. I am angry at myself for not buying him the puzzle when we were at the museum; this was a fun, appropriate gift for him, and your anger at Dad and me for picking it out was strange. To me, this issue is important. I would like to ask you to do two things that I think will start to work it out: 1. buy a copy of the puzzle and send it to Lyle and 2. figure out a plan for taking him on a trip comparable to the trip you are starting to plan with Myra.

Sincerely,
Allen

By confronting the past and understanding his role in perpetuating bad patterns in his family, Allen has effected change not only in his relationship with his sister but with the entire family, and this change will change how his parents interact with his children as well as how he interacts with them.

....

Katie had given up trying to stop her mother from constantly carping at her, but the position she was left in with her mother made her relationship with her brother troublesome. He did not understand or acknowledge that her relationship with their mother was different from his. This created a barrier between them. Here is Katie's letter to her brother:

Dear Griff,

I felt sad when I left you after breakfast the other morning. Often with you I want to feel closer, be more personal, and don't know how to go about it. It seems even harder since Mother got sick. Before then I think it was easier for you to believe that your experience with her was very different from mine. I feel now that you would defend her if I were to talk with you about something she has done to me—that you wouldn't believe my perspective on it. You are more tolerant of Mother's difficult behavior than I am, but you have a stronger and more solid bond with her than I do.

I'm sure you find it hard to believe that she never says one single complimentary comment about my work—in the years I've been doing the Newsletter (and I have people all over the state asking for it), the only comments she has made were, once, that it was printed crookedly and once she asked what was the point of protesting to Blue Cross. The only thing I can ever remember Mother praising me for was sewing. She is almost always covertly critical. Last time she came to dinner, the whole family was chuckling after she left about the number of times she mentioned how to cook broccoli the "right" way. No matter how well I understand the dynamics of this—her own sense of guilt about me and her competitiveness with me—on a day-to-day basis it's hard to live with.

If I hadn't always loved you so much myself, it would have created a pretty fierce competition between us. Perhaps my own admiration for you gets in the way of us being closer, too.

All I want is for you to recognize that, even if she's sick,
Mother is capable of treating me very nastily, so I don't feel
such a barrier between you and me. And I wish we could know
each other better. I have always loved you.

Katie

Katie's letter was too nice to be effective. It took about a year
for her to realize how writing and sending the letter had not
worked to change her feelings. Her brother was still so allied with
their mother that he failed to notice how badly she treated Katie.
He still admonished Katie for not being kind to her. Katie remained angry at Griff.

She wrote him again. Although she mentioned her anger at
Griff, she focused her negative feelings on their mother. After
complaining about their mother, she covered her negative feelings about Griff by offering him advice about his depression. She
knew, even before she sent the letter, that she had not been honest. Katie wrote a third letter and brought it into her group for
feedback. In this letter she finally reveals what prevents her from
being herself with her brother. She still does not address her
anger at Griff directly, but at least she tells him what she has discovered through the writing process that has kept her from being
closer to him.

Dear Griff,

I have been working with a memory, one of the few early
memories I have. It's very clear and very powerful. We were in
Australia. I was four years old so you would then have been
nine. We were on the stairs, I was in my pajamas, and I believe
Mother and Daddy were going out for the evening. You said,
"Who do you love most, Mother or Daddy?" I was dumb-
founded. It had never occurred to me that I might love one

more than the other. It was that "aha" experience in which I was suddenly faced with the realization that my parents were not perfect creatures, that there was enough of a difference that one could *choose between them. Before I could respond you said, "Of course you love Mother more, don't you?" You were so certain, and my big brother, after all. I think at that moment (totally unbeknownst to you) I decided that (1) there was something "wrong" with loving Daddy, and (2) I was going to have to keep quiet about it, or I might lose your love.*

It seems like I've spent the rest of my life keeping myself hidden, not standing up for what I thought, or how I felt, acting as though I had no value, afraid of not being loved.

I'm writing to say that I loved Daddy more because he loved me more. I'm sorry he was so mean to you. I'm sorry that the family belief system was that he was useless because that made his loving me have no value. Forty-six years old and still struggling with this shit.

Mother says that my presents for her are so impersonal. I gave her some Peppermint Foot Lotion, for her calluses, that I have used the last several weeks that have softened my feet so that they no longer crack and bleed, which I know hers do, too. She said she might try it in the fall.

Love,
Katie

Just when it looks as if she is going to be openly angry with Griff, Katie sidetracks. She first turns her anger on herself ("Forty-six years old and still struggling with this shit") and then complains that her mother never appreciates her gifts. In this way she hides her anger at her brother for not being sympathetic about how mean their mother is to Katie. Writing this draft made Katie see that part of her anger has to do with her dashed expectation that her brother would be particularly sympathetic, given his own experience of being treated unfairly by their father.

Katie plans to rewrite the last two paragraphs of the letter to express her anger at Griff and to acknowledge how envious and competitive she feels toward him because his ally lived and hers died. This rewrite will not be easy, but Katie has paced each letter according to what she feels ready to express; each time she writes and gets feedback, she gains insight into herself, her brother, and the family dynamics. The writing process has shown her how hard it is for her to be honest with her anger and the problems that this creates for her. Interestingly, since working on these letters to her brother, Katie has been less willing to accept her mother's constant criticisms and more able to cut her mother off when her mother starts up. Her mother has responded by being a little less critical.

8

Confronting the Secret

SEXUAL ABUSE BY CARETAKERS

Often the victim of abuse is so traumatized and has dissociated from or repressed so much of his experience that when he becomes more aware of the traumatic material, it generates a post-traumatic stress-like reaction in which guilt is recreated along with the original pain and trauma.

Merely contemplating a direct confrontation of the abuser can terrorize the potential confronter. If this happens, there is no chance for communication, but if the victim of abuse can write a letter that he knows does not have to be sent, the process of composing the letter and revising it provides the time, safety, and distance to overcome the terror. The timing can be finely adjusted. The writer can decide not to send the letter until he has gotten enough internal psychological strength and/or external support so that, even if the worst-case predictions come true, he is ready on his own timetable. He can rehearse options and prepare how to react to different imagined responses. In these ways, the writer can gain control and reduce his terror of confronting the abuser.

There are, of course, cases such as Dr. B.'s where the sexual abuse is so blatant or continues to an advanced enough age that the victim has never denied or minimized the experience. In such cases the abused person has often kept the abuse secret because of her shame and because of her desire to protect the abuser. Sometimes the abuser is also the only person who was ever sympathetic or kind to her.

Often, though, there is so much dissociation and denial that the client and/or therapist doubt whether a specific abuse happened. In this age of victim popularity, such a doubt can be healthy skepticism or it can be further harmful denial and dissociation from reality. The response to the letter home can settle the matter, as often happens when the responder acknowledges the abuse and defends it or tries to bribe the writer to keep it secret. This verification of reality can be extremely important for getting well.

Lorna first called her older brother because she was having memories of being sexually molested by his friends. He readily confirmed that her memory was correct and said he too had been sexual with her since she was a small child. It was soon after this that Lorna remembered (in detail) that her father had been sexual with her, too. She wrote the following letter to her parents and brother:

> *Dear mother, father, and brother,*
>
> *I am writing you to request that you assume responsibility for the cost of my psychotherapy. For the last ten years, I have worked hard to overcome the problems your sexual, physical, and emotional abuse has caused me. You can pay. I have paid long enough.*

Despite these many years of therapy and the changes I have been able to make in my life, I have continued to suffer because of my successes in work and love. In 1985 I was hospitalized twice for suicidal depression. At that time I was finishing my dissertation and about to receive my Ph.D. in recognition for my hard work, my research, and scholarship. This was a big milestone in my life, yet I nearly killed myself rather than rejoice. Every time I feel good about myself, proud of something I've accomplished, I feel I am in danger. The beginning of this year was another milestone—my boyfriend and I talked about sharing a life together. I immediately had an experience similar to the one in 1985.

The real danger for me is not in the present but in the past I suppressed to avoid the knowledge that you willfully crippled and abused me. Now I am the abuser who will not let me have a life of my own, not let me appreciate my own talents and gifts, who has a hard time believing anyone genuinely cares for me, that anyone can be trusted. Now I know why this is. This year instead of trying to kill myself, I was ready to face what really happened to me. The only way to heal myself was to uncover past memories that I had blocked to the point that I did not remember much of my childhood.

I have spent the last six months excavating my childhood and living with the memories I uncovered. They keep on coming.

From a very early age, I knew that no one was in charge, that no one was there to protect me or had my best interest at heart. You mother left me in Marvin's care when I was a baby and he was just four years old. I was taking care of my baby brother at the same age. You both talked of this as if it were perfectly normal for four-year-olds to take care of infants and toddlers.

But that is not all. You did not protect me from the sexual abuse I was subjected to by Mr. K., Daddy, Marvin, and possibly others as well. You knew about all of this, yet you did nothing. I remember one time telling you about my brother Marvin and my cousin. You were in the kitchen cooking. I came in holding my hands and shaking and told you. You never said a word. You acted as though you didn't hear me. I ran into the woods because I was safer there than at home. Marvin remembers that I had told on him before the incident with him and Lonnie. He said you told Daddy and Daddy reprimanded him by threatening to lock him up (jail, reformatory). Then the matter was dropped and Marvin kept putting his hands in my pants and masturbating on me at the same time Daddy was also abusing me. I had no one to turn to for protection.

I had to protect myself from you as well as Dad and my brother. You poisoned all my friendships by telling me those people were just out to use me. That was your truth about you, not them. In fact, you tried to destroy everything in my life that did not revolve around you.

And revolve around you I did. In order to get any attention from you, I had to give up my childhood to take care of you— listen to your problems, take care of my younger brothers and sister, keep Daddy happy. I was very perceptive about your needs as well as Daddy's and learned to gain favor by serving your interests. I had to hide myself away and be very careful to only mirror you (not show I was a child) just to survive.

You did not allow us to be children who needed to be nurtured as unique individuals, people with our own gifts and talents. When I was eight or nine I said something to this effect at the dinner table, "Why can't we live decent like other people instead of like a bunch of hogs rooting at the trough?" You slapped me several times trying to shut me up. To me at that time "decent" meant being nurtured and respected for who we were. . . . In fact, your answer to my question was to get Dad to beat me up.

You, Dad, did more than hit. You molested me from the time I was four years old through my adolescence. I remember when I was only four or five, you used to take me to the barn on Sunday afternoons. I know it was Sunday because I still had on my patent leather shoes and a frilly dress with a sash on it. You would show me things in the barn, like the big king snake. Then you would ask me if I would like to see something else. You picked me up and laid me face down on a barrel and pulled my pants down around my ankles and ran your penis over my legs. I was so scared I was shaking and had trouble catching my breath. You kept on asking me if it felt good and I said yes. I knew better than to say no. You would get mad and leave me. You asked me again as you lifted me up and put your penis between my legs. You pumped my body faster and faster, forcing me to say yes it felt good until you climaxed. You then wiped off my legs and stomach, pulled up my pants and lifted me off the barrel on to your knee. You ran your hand all over me and said, "Now don't tell Mama about what we did. She would be jealous and mad if she knew I did this with you." I never did tell, not then at four when you called me your little princess and I believed I was special.

I thought I had saved myself from your physical abuse because you and I had this fantasy thing going about me being a princess. But you beat me up when Mama told you to. You beat me for being smart, for being visible, for having opinions that did not agree with yours and Mama's. I remember when I was nine or ten you whipping me and saying, "You think you're so smart. I'll show you who's smart." I was heartbroken. I remember standing while you whipped my legs, sobbing. I grabbed

*your legs and pleaded with you to stop. You stooped down, put
your arm around me, and said, "I hate to have to whip my little girl but you shouldn't talk to your Mama like that." Then
you put your hand in my pants. Later you unzipped your
britches and told me to kiss your penis. I did. You told me to
suck your penis. I did, but I wouldn't put it in my mouth like
you wanted me to. So you zipped your britches up and went
away cold and mad. You were the only one I thought cared
about me, talked to me, shared things with me. I would do
anything to maintain my connection with you. So, I finally did
what you wanted me to do, later on.*

*As for you, Marvin, your sexual abuse started when I was
seven or eight years old. I already had some of the memories of
you molesting me as a teenager, and you told me the rest in our
phone conversation. You said when you put your hands in my
pants or masturbated on me, I never said a word, never moved.
It was like I wasn't even there. By that time at age seven I was
already being molested by Daddy and had been molested by
Mr. K., and had already learned that no one was going to protect me. The only way I could protect myself was to dissociate,
go to some fantasy place in my head. There, I was a ballerina
dancing on the stage, proud of my strong, beautiful body, and
admired and respected for my talent.*

*To you, Marvin, I was just a female body to be used for your
adolescent male ego. You were more concerned about proving
yourself to Lonnie than you were about what you were doing
to your little sister. When we talked on the phone, the only
thing that seemed to bother you about molesting me was that I
was your sister. You made some comment about turning "in-
ward" with your sexual activity, rather than "outward." You saw
no difference between molesting a defenseless child (sister or*

no sister) and experimenting with a girl your own age who was willing.

After this conversation, you called again on my birthday. I very clearly stated that I did not want to talk with you at this time. . . . But you wouldn't take no for an answer. You called several times a day for a week. You still violate and intrude on very clear boundaries I set for my protection.

By the time I was twelve, I did not want to live anymore. All three of you had robbed me of my childhood and my self-respect. You made me feel dirty and ashamed. I did not know my life could get any worse, but it did. You, mother, expected me to take more responsibility for the house and the rest of the kids. I was only thirteen when you taught me how to drive so that I could run errands for you. You shared with me your depressing views of womanhood as one long trial of suffering and self-sacrifice. That was already my life, but I swore it wouldn't be when I left home. . . .

As a teenager, I was shamed by the lack of respect both you and Daddy showed toward your own bodies and ours. You, Daddy, would walk around the house with nothing on but your undershirt exposing your behind and covering your genitals with your hand and shirt. You, mother, used to call me into the bathroom where you sat naked and legs open wide on the toilet with your whole crotch exposed. You also gave me enemas ostensibly for constipation. I have never had problems with constipation. I feel just as violated by you as I do by Mr. K., Daddy, and Marvin.

And you, Dad, wanted to have intercourse, now that I was a "woman." This scared me because I could become pregnant and trapped with you two forever. I think I would have killed myself first. I tried to appease you with other things. One time

I let you take off my clothes and place me on the rug in the living room. You tried to put your penis in my rectum, but it was too painful. I asked you to stop. I collapsed on the floor and curled up in a fetal position and lay there crying. You slapped me lightly on my ass as you left the room and said, "It hurts a little at first but you will get used to it. You will even like it."

I knew at that moment the truth about you and Mother. You were both screwing me with my help. I had sacrificed all my life trying to get your love. I knew then that the only thing that would happen to me if I continued to let both of you have your way with me is that I would end up in the back ward of a mental institution or be so broken that the only thing I would be good for is caring for you the rest of my life. . . .

I decided I would not give in and give up without a fight. I pulled out all the stops. I ran around with hoodlums, carried switchblades, destroyed public property, skipped school, and drank beer. I had violent fights with both of you. I had the reputation as a "bad kid." And that looked real bad for you because you were leaders in the church. That was my weapon. I was willing to do anything to embarrass you, I threatened to spill the beans on the things I could remember that you, Dad, had done to my older brother. I also wanted to scare and intimidate you so that you would leave me alone. The only peace I got was spending more and more time in the woods by myself.

I was still a needy kid. Dad, you and I were midnight lovers while Mama worked the night shift. I never did make a total break with you, but I, at least, wanted to scare you and find some proof that you cared about me as a person. I used to walk the road at one and two o'clock in the morning. You caught me at least once and gave me this pierced, hurt look, as I came upon you waiting for me out in the yard. You showed me how to waltz. You pointed out the constellations of stars to me, yet you hurt and abused me at the same time.

There were dangers everywhere—at home with you three and out on the streets with my hoodlum friends. The girls were getting pregnant. The boys were going to jail. I did not intend to end up like that. I had a few allies—teachers, beyond the inferno you two created for me.

But it took more than leaving home to leave you behind. The way you treated me influenced my view of the world, the way I treated others, my ability to do creative work. Yet the more I succeeded, the more I suffered and the more I abused others who loved me and tried to help me. Now I know why. The last six months have been devoted totally to reconstructing my past. With the help of my therapists, my employer, my boyfriend, and friends (some of whom are also survivors of sexual and physical abuse), I have faced the pain and the grief for my lost childhood.

With each new revelation about what you did to me, I was amazed at my own resolve and strength as a child and an adolescent to have survived your abuse. It is in that same spirit of strength and courage that I confront you now so that I can heal myself and trust my own spirit and inner voice. All these years, I have protected you with my silence. No longer.

Now you have the opportunity to claim responsibility for your actions, if you are strong enough. The choice is yours.

Please do not call me. If you want to communicate, write a letter. I do not wish to talk with you at this time. Consider my outstanding loans your small contributions to my therapy costs. The cost for therapy over the last ten years is listed on the next page.

Lorna

Lorna enclosed a list of therapy costs indicating what insurance paid and what she held them responsible for. Included was a cover letter from a lawyer saying they could remit the money to her via him or to her directly. As a result of Lorna's letter home, her parents and brother made no attempt to deny the abuse. They immediately paid her past therapy expenses.

Long before the sexual abuse was uncovered, Lorna was aware that whenever she felt particularly trusting about a relationship, she assumed betrayal, pain, and suffering would follow, as it had in her family.

What we observed in her therapy group was that whenever we were particularly helpful, Lorna would come to the next session enraged and especially hostile to the person she had felt closest to in the previous session. She did this to me so often that I told her that if I knew her other than as a client there was no way I would have anything more to do with her and her abusive behavior. I said I was sick of her biting the hand that fed her and that the only reason I was hanging in was that I was her therapist and it was my responsibility. My confrontation had a profound impact on her; it jolted her into seeing how compelled she was to repeat old patterns.

As Lorna's dynamics unfolded, her behavior made more sense. Always mistreating the person she felt closest to left her in control of the expected betrayal and abandonment. She did not have to wait for something bad to happen. She could cause it to happen, get it over with, and hurt the person who, in the old script, would have betrayed her trust. When she could not play this out with her therapists, other authorities, fellow group members, or peers, she would internalize the abusive father/brother/mother and mistreat herself for hours at a time: obsessively telling herself how bad she was, reviewing in detail painful thoughts and feelings, and then drinking until she passed out.

Lorna did not have to cut off her family. After they paid her therapy bills (they were afraid she would expose them), they made little effort to contact her. She is not yet "cured" of the desire to undermine herself or those who help her. Most of the time, though, she catches herself before she acts out this old script. She is more able to tolerate good things happening to her and to stop herself from destructive behavior.

An abused person is often connected to the abuser by fantasies of revenge. These fantasies are related to feelings of powerlessness that the victim has because she was once a child totally dependent on the abuser. The need for revenge keeps her tied up in the past, still dependent on the old parent demon. The letter, as in Lorna's case, can be a form of healthy revenge— healthy because it enables her to move into constructive action instead of staying with destructive passivity or wishful thinking. The writer can finally close the circle of unresolved feelings: expose the secret, break the silence, and claim power.

....

Therapists, like parents, are supposed to be caretakers. Therapists, like parents, sometimes misuse their role. I include a letter from Beth. She kept the abuse by her former therapist secret throughout many years of therapy with me, even when I confronted her with my suspicions. The therapist, like many parents, may have been nurturing and protective as well as abusive. This creates a conflict for the client. A need to protect the abuser and to keep the good nurturing part of the relationship intact comes into agonizing conflict with the need to protect oneself. This conflict is expressed clearly by Beth in her letter to her former therapist, which she wrote after finally admitting to me that they had a sexual relationship:

Dear Raymond,

This letter is long overdue, but I have just arrived at the point of being able to write it.

I need to express to you how our affair, and my keeping it a secret all these years to protect you, has damaged me and prolonged the course of my therapy. I participated willingly; I am partly to blame. But I consider you mostly to blame; you are a professional therapist who had the responsibility to know better and to control your emotions.

As I have told you before, I felt very grateful for your caring, intelligent therapeutic attention when I first came to you. I did feel that you saved my life. Part of the reason I was such an emotional mess then was—as you know—a direct result of the affair I had had with the psychiatrist who treated me when I was hospitalized for suicidal depression ten years earlier.

Our affair began just after I left therapy with you and went, at your urging, to another therapist. . . . I consider the timing of the affair a technicality; your seductiveness began long before I left therapy with you, and afterward you were still, in my mind, my therapist. You expressed some concern about that at the beginning of the affair; you should have paid more attention to your misgivings. But I think you (to put it in the kindest light possible) deluded yourself even before that, while I was still in therapy with you. You once proposed, when I was your patient, that you adopt me as your child—this new, healthy reparenting, according to some California shrink, was to give me the solid emotional base I was lacking from my childhood. I remember being very excited about this (in a curious way, I now realize). Then you told me it couldn't be done because of your wife's objection; she felt threatened by me, you told me. In hindsight, I am not surprised that she knew about your feelings—but why didn't you pay atten-

tion to them? I am glad that she objected to that plan, which would have been a grotesque replaying of my original family situation.

As you well knew—after all, we worked and worked on it— a major root of my psychological problems was my unhealthy relationship with my father, and the guilt I felt about it. You, more than anyone, should have been aware that I would be (and was) acting out that Oedipal connection in a physical relationship with you, my therapist-father. Because of the affair, my guilty secret, I have for years prolonged and intensified my internal scraping—punishing myself in all sorts of ways, because I felt I deserved it.

You claimed, throughout the affair, to love me passionately. Your marriage, you intimated, was but a pale imitation of our relationship. You said disparaging things about your wife (shades of my father!). Yet you were always fanatic about keeping our relationship secret. We did not even have intercourse because of your fear that I might become pregnant.

I ended our affair after your wife became pregnant. Our close relationship continued for a while under the guise of our working together on a writing project. When I did end our affair, you were at first angry. Then you said that you recognized my act as a sign that I was really healthy. So you did admit that our relationship was harmful to me.

All along—and especially after our affair ended—you had me vow to keep it secret, even in my (current) therapy. I have for years protected you, at great expense to myself . . . you treated me very badly. You involved me in an affair which you had to know was poison for me. You lied to me. You had me damage myself in order to protect your precious reputation. The cost to me has been very large—in pain, in lost time, in money spent on therapy.

*I also feel a responsibility toward other of your female pa-
tients whom you might similarly damage.*

*I do not know what I will do about these feelings. I will let
you know when I decide.*

Beth

After writing this letter, Beth decided to ask for reimbursement
of all the money she had paid Raymond for therapy. He reimbursed
her and called me in an effort to get me to understand. (He had referred her to me and had known for a long time that I was suspicious about his relationship with Beth because, despite his repeated
denials, I had continued to confront him with my suspicions.)

Before writing this letter, Beth routinely contaminated pleasure with pain. She felt so guilty whenever she felt pleasure that
she needed to punish herself. She often felt suicidal. Writing the
letter freed her from her incestuous script. Beth understands
how her therapist/father helped her as well as harmed her and
how she was in part responsible for the harm. In writing this letter she not only ceased to be a victim, she became fully responsible for taking care of herself. Beth's brave confrontation helped
other current and potential victims. Her letter was used to start
proceedings that would prevent her former therapist from abusing more patients (he had already abused several other patients)
and ensure that he would get help himself.

A major consequence of having written this letter is that Beth
now feels entitled to her pleasure. Even though her life as a single working mother is often very difficult, she maintains her equilibrium and finds pleasure in ordinary activities.

....

Nancy was in therapy years before she uncovered her feelings
about her mother and her mother's role in the family pattern of

sexual and emotional abuse. Once the pattern became clear to her she tried to talk to her mother, but when she was with her mother Nancy became protective and was able to voice only innocuous and vague criticisms. The task of really communicating with her mother seemed enormous. Nancy determined to say everything in a letter and decide later whether she had the courage to send it. Her letter did say everything.

Dear Mama,

I've been so angry at you for so many long years that the feelings I shared during our previous talk were only the surface layer of an enormous ocean of pain, grief, and self-loathing.

You sacrificed and betrayed me much earlier than when I was pregnant at fifteen . . . you set me up to sleep with Daddy those months when you were in bed with your back. I pleaded with you not to, but you made me become your stand-in . . . I think to appease him while you were sick. That incestuous relationship and your total abandonment of me for your own self-interest caused me irreparable damage that changed the whole course of my life.

What I lost in that experience was my sense of being a person of value and my belief that my parents would protect me. I lost owning my own body, and I lost the ability to say no to unwanted touching. . . . I was a set-up for a relationship that had no love or caring in it. I never wanted to have sex with Clint [her boyfriend whom she later married], I was raped that first time . . . but I had no one I trusted to turn to for help. The more I allowed sex with him the more devalued I felt, so that eventually I believed I was very very bad and deserved the beatings he gave me. It was really me beating myself. When I became pregnant, you forced me to go live with a violent, volatile seventeen year old boy who continued to brutalize me emo-

tionally and physically. I think you were relieved to have me
out of your house.

After my son was born, you let both of us go back with Clint,
not only me, but a helpless baby with teenagers for parents.
During the time that Clint, my son, and I lived in Virginia . . .
you could see my weight loss, lethargy, despondency . . . you
didn't help me look at other options. It was my own survival
instinct and the neighbors who got me out of there, not you.

When Clint called us at home to say he was coming to get
my son and me with a gun, I told you I believed he was capable of killing me and so did you . . . Other mothers would have
taken their family to safety and let the police handle it. But—
not causing a scene in front of the neighbors was more important than protecting the lives of your children and grandchild.

After my daughter was born, you wanted me to get a job
without finishing school. It was me that wanted to go back in
spite of my socially embarrassing background. . . .

When I became pregnant for the third time, I told you I was
going to take quinine to abort the baby. . . . When the quinine
didn't produce an abortion, once again there was no talk of options that were safe other than being sent away again and making up a ridiculous lie in an attempt to keep up appearances.

At last you sent me to a psychiatrist who said I was using sex
as a way to get love. He was right, Mama. And yet both you
and Daddy exclaimed amazement at that possibility. I must be
crazy to not know that you both loved me, and the whole matter was dropped. You never saw that sex was the only way I
thought I had to get anything. My history was screaming that
out to you, but it was easier for you to ignore and deny than to
acknowledge your part in the whole thing.

When I came back home again, you wanted me to look for
a job without finishing school. Just like the first time, I went

*back to high school after my daughter was born. You wanted
me to be a secretary. What kind of mother has such low aspirations for such a bright child? I think one who doesn't want
the child to have a better life than herself. I think you didn't
want to face what you had settled for in your own life.*

*I chose not to settle for low aspirations. . . . When I went
away to law school, I began to redefine myself. I modeled myself on my friend Sara, on the ways she placed high value on
her needs, her behavior, on the way she required others, especially men, to treat her—that and a new-found competency in
school is what started me on the road again.*

*Mama, because the feeling that you abandoned me time
and time again was so painful, I chose to change that feeling
to one I had control over—I believed I was a very bad person
to my long-suffering Christian mother. . . . Surely you must be
a good person since you cared so much for the environment,
the downtrodden, for fairness and justice in the world, you
never cursed or took the Lord's name in vain, were always "sacrificing" yourself for your family—surely a person like that
would not do harm to her child. That is an admirable person,
that kind of sensitive mother must love me enough to do what's
good for me, therefore I must be the bad one. I must be the selfish one doing these things to my patient, martyred mother. But
Mama, I was the one who found a way to save myself each
time, and you were the one who tried to keep me down.*

Nancy

Before Nancy got the nerve to send the letter, her mother had
a stroke. Nancy knew it was unlikely that her mother would live
much longer. She decided to read her letter to her mother in the
hospital even though her mother was comatose. When she read
the letter, Nancy could not even tell whether her mother could

hear her, but she experienced relief that she had at least read it to her. After her mother died, she shared the letter with her brothers and sisters and her children.

Nancy showed her son the letter, and this led to his disclosure that he was sexually molested by his aunt (Nancy's sister). He was immensely relieved to tell his mother. They pledged to continue to talk openly. She began to suspect that her now grown daughter's symptoms—eating disorder, phobias, panic attacks, and strange attitudes about her body—might be the result of sexual abuse. She suspected her brother Mark and her long dead father.

The cover letter Nancy sent to Mark gives an idea of how one confronting letter to a parent can open up a previously closed family system in which every member has agreed to keep silent about what he or she knows.

Dear Mark,

I've worked a long time on the enclosed letter to Mama. I was planning to send it to her after the weekend at the lake, but she had the stroke. I did read it to her while she was comatose and was able to let out some of the anger and sadness, but I never got her response to it. I waited too long because I was afraid. . . .

I want to share this with you because I want to stop living in the family tradition of remaining silent about real issues. I want to stop pretending that we're close to each other when each of us has a barrier a mile thick. I want more from my brothers and sister, but I'm still afraid of having more. It's hard for me to tell what your take is on our family, and I want your honest response. I hope this letter will be another step toward drawing closer. I've really noticed and liked your reaching out and trying.

Nancy

When Mark responded positively both to Nancy's letter to her mother and to her cover letter to him, Nancy invited him in for a joint therapy session. During the session he admitted that he had frequently hit his niece but denied having any sexual contact with her. He then confessed to sexually abusing his younger siste with a group of his friends. More and more incestuous secrets emerged. Having the courage to confront one's own abuse often encourages the confronter to deal with how she has carried on bad family dynamics by abusing others. Nancy and Mark went on to explore the web of incestuous relationships in the family, what role each of them played, and how it affected them in terms of raising their children and in terms of their own (lack of) sexual boundaries and identity. They were very open with each other. They talked about the barriers each of them put up to avoid being close to the other and possible causes for these barriers, including the fear that they might become sexual with each other if they were emotionally close.

Her daughter is the only member of the family who refuses to read the letter Nancy wrote to her mother. Nancy has given her daughter a copy and told her to read it when she feels ready.

Sometimes after a series of letter exchanges, the writer and recipient can meet face to face. By then the worst, the hardest part, is usually over. In Nancy's case this was impossible because her mother died, but she did the next best thing and met with everyone else in the family.

There are new possibilities for family healing and closeness because of Nancy's courage and leadership. Each of her brothers and her sister revealed other family secrets. We will never know, of course, whether Nancy would have had as much support and openness from her brothers and sister if her mother and father were not already dead.

Breaking the silence, exposing secrets that have been destructive to growth and happiness, is one of the primary functions of confrontational letter writing. Sometimes a letter is the first exposure of a family script for generations and so carries with it the potential to change future generations.

9

Confronting the Elusive

COVERT ABUSE

It is a truism among therapists that covert abuse is often more damaging to a child's development than overt abuse, in part because it is so much more difficult for the victim to figure out. A father who gets angry and violent when he is drunk and beats the children does not cause them as much long-term psychological damage as the father who mocks the children and then kisses and fondles them telling them how sorry he is and how much he loves them, or how much closer he feels to them than he does to his wife. A mother who is openly critical of her daughter, even vicious to her, is not as destructive as a mother who acts loving but is jealous of her husband's attentions to her child and competitive with that child. This latter mother might not berate her daughter herself. She may instead set her daughter up to be criticized by the father and then comfort the daughter, telling her that she loves her and that the father does not love her.

When people grow up in families where there are big differences between the overt and the covert, between what is said and
what is really happening, the discrepancy between the surface
and what goes on underneath confuses them. They doubt their
own feelings and perceptions. Confidence in the value of feelings
as an indicator for action is inhibited. These people grow up to be
adults who have a hard time giving and receiving love and a hard
time knowing how to trust.

Mary's mother wanted the best for Mary. Nevertheless, she
had a covertly damaging effect on Mary's emotional development. Mary, an only child, was very aware of the unhealthy relationships in her family. She understood and took responsibility
for her role as a daughter who excluded her mother, was seductive with her father, and got sick or maximized illnesses to gain attention. She was able to see what roles her mother and father
played in the family pathology. Even working this out in therapy,
though, did not dislodge the punitive mother that Mary had internalized as a grown woman.

Her internal mother, what Mary and her therapy group came
to call her Mother Harpy, was never satisfied, always disdainful.
Mary wrote the following letter to her mother to try to break
down the barriers between them so that she could stop torturing
herself with the worst parts of her mother.

Dear Mom,

*I needed to write you this letter to define the negative as-
pects of myself that I got from you. These parts of me are now
an authentic part of myself, but I want to change them. This
letter is not meant to push you away or cut you off—I hope
writing to you makes it easier, not harder, for us to have a real
connection.*

The first words I speak or think in the morning when I get up are "I hate myself." They come out, out loud, during the day, too, when I think of something I'm embarrassed about and won't forget or forgive myself for. I have taken on the constant disapproval you made me feel for myself. The constant critical eye. You were watching over me, judging all the time, and I never lived up. I pick at myself; my mind is always "at" me.

I have a hard time just being myself, knowing what that is. You were so controlling, it took me forever to get my own self. You wouldn't let me be different from your idea, your image of me. You wouldn't let me be different from you, or even just different. I was like your house. I had to be perfect. (I wish you hadn't tried so hard to make my panties match my dress—so much trouble.)

I do your scowl, your sneer, at anyone else who has fantasy and is different. I'm jealous of their fantasy. (A friend who wore an unusual but not inappropriate dress to an occasion— I looked at her and scowled. She could feel my disdain. Really I wished I could be more like her. And you sneered at the pictures of Pierre and Nannette, Pierre with a beard, judging them so superficially—they are among my closest and most cherished friends.)

I'm rigid just like you. I have to control my environment. I'm afraid of risk. Cal used to go through Hell before we'd do anything daring and fun because I was nervous and would whine and complain. So I prefer to deal with my fears silently and alone.

I'm so hard on myself. I don't know how to play without feeling guilty. (Me waiting for Susie McPherson to pick me up; you say: "Don't you have something you can get working on so you don't waste your time?") I overdo what I'm "sup-

posed" to do and don't get to the fun things that I'd like to do. I give too much of myself at the university because I'm so wedded to obligations (as you used to invite people for dinner not because you liked them but because you were obligated).

I can't accept and enjoy the fact that I'm intelligent; I'm constantly overworking to prove that I am smart enough to be where I am. I think you're smart, too, but I also think you were jealous or intimidated by my smarts and punished me when I used my comebacks to get back at you for controlling my life. . . .

I have trouble showing affection. In fact, I "bite the hand that feeds me." Many of the ways you showed affection had a double edge: controlling and negative.

I dislike my own body and am scared of and disgusted by sex. My body smells and is nasty. (You smelled my underpants and made me feel that normal secretions were bad, and the doctor reinforced that sex would hurt, I'd have to be "stretched" before getting married. Which was untrue.) I suspect that you were cold to Dad or he took the easy way out because his attentions to me were often inappropriate—a swipe on the ass as a teenager when I came through the room. Why didn't he do that to you? . . .

I got the general message from you that I'm bad, nasty, and selfish. I don't need you to tell me these negative things anymore because I do it to myself.

I'd like your reactions to my letter in writing or if it's easier for you—talk into a tape—but not a phone call. It's too easy to be misunderstood—and not to have time to listen in a phone call.

I'll look forward to hearing from you.

Love,
Mary

We grow up internalizing parental messages and play them back to ourselves. Mary's letter to her mother highlights the potency of parental messages—in this case, negative messages. These messages were repeated and therefore reinforced each time Mary saw or spoke to her mother. The negative messages are usually formed from the parent's own insecurities and fears projected onto the child. Mary's mother felt socially insecure. She had little self-esteem, worried about her intellect, and was afraid of intimacy and sexuality.

Like many parents, her mother was attempting to shape her daughter to help her avoid some of the pain that she had experienced when she was growing up. Mary's mother projected herself onto her daughter, failing to respect her daughter as a separate person.

Whenever Mary talked to her mother, she ended up feeling that she was bad, nasty, and selfish. Even when an interaction with her mother was largely positive, Mary would scan for the negative and absorb only the negative messages. She didn't even need verbal messages; she would pick up a look, sound, or gesture that would convey the negative message. She was so exquisitely sensitive to negative cues that in the space of a few minutes' conversation Mary would absorb so many negative messages that she would feel demoralized, angry, and confirmed in her view of her mother and of herself. The way I see it, it's as if Mary's Mother Harpy became bigger and stronger each time Mary interacted with her mother.

Putting her understanding of the origins and character of her Mother Harpy on paper had the effect of "outing" her Harpy. Mary had finally openly blamed her mother for the origin of the Harpy and her negative view of herself. She could then take responsibility for internalizing these negative messages: "I don't need you to tell me these negative things anymore because I do it to myself."

Because the process was now conscious for both Mary and her mother, Mary's mother made some efforts (which she could not in the long run sustain) to stop transmitting her negative projections onto Mary. More importantly, Mary's letter home gave her greater control over whether she absorbed such messages and enabled her to counter these negative distortions with reality. This has lessened Mary's animosity toward her mother and toward herself.

....

It took Dean some years in group therapy to understand what it was that kept him repeating old patterns with bosses, friends, and lovers and with his grown children. Getting clear involved untangling the mostly covert undercurrents that went on in his family of origin. During this time he wrote to his father:

Dear Dad:

One of the things that has become clear to me about you and me is that you were not there for me when I needed you. Mom had her own hang-ups, which you know better than I, but I needed you to help me break the bond between me and Mom. She was not willing to give me the necessary firm, gentle push away from her as I grew up.

You were capable. You were a great model for loving the outdoors and using reference books and being a helpmate to your wife, and persevering. However, you never told her to keep her hands off of me when she was drunk. Do you have any idea how humiliating it was for me to have her talk about my penis to my dates? Or have her suggestively crawl into my sleeping bag while she was drunk? I tried to cop a feel and she screamed *to you that I was pinching her. I couldn't win for losing. I might have been eleven years old.*

. . . My accusation is that you didn't want to help me get away from her because I was a distraction for her while you worked.

You never took me by the hand and said, "What is wrong with you? You are smart, and you bring home C's and D's." You saw the whiskey bottles on my dresser but refused to say, "I don't want you to drink that shit. It will kill you and I love you. Your teachers tell me you are a clown and a distraction in school. What is going on?" The only advice you ever gave me about women was that you would rather I bought a piece than get a girl pregnant and that women are hard to deal with when they are having their period.

The reason I never felt like I could tell you any of these things is that you disappear when confronted with anger, sadness, and probably love.

Dean

Dean was relieved that he had put his feelings down on paper and had the guts to send them to his father. When he received a defensive, unsatisfactory response letter, he sent a few other letters, but to no avail. The major result of the exchange was that Dean felt a little less dependent on his father.

When Dean terminated group therapy, he had no idea that he would be back several years later feeling mired in the vain hope that his parents would recognize and acknowledge their problems (his mom's alcoholism and sexualized interactions with him, for example, and his dad's neglect) and the destructive consequences of their behavior in their son's life. Given his parents' previous self-serving, defensive responses, he knew this acknowledgment would not be forthcoming, and he knew that he would not get any credit for his accomplishments. He stayed angry at them and therefore focused on them and their behavior and faults instead of focusing on his own goals. He worked in group to unhook himself from his need for his parents' approval. Dean wrote one more letter to give himself closure on his feelings about his parents:

Dear Mom and Dad:

I want you to hear this. You missed it the last time I tried to tell you about it six years ago, and in the process I felt belittled and libeled by you for bringing it up.

I have had a hard time growing up into a happy, responsible adult. . . . I have labored with a lack of self-confidence, with self-destructiveness, and a terror of being left by my intimates. I am not being melodramatic, this is who I have been for much of my life. I have been more comfortable with seduction, outbursts of violence, deceit, and invisibility than with honest, open interchange. I have gotten along by ingratiating myself to others and consequently spent many years living in icy cold self-loathing for not having the courage of my own convictions. I am better equipped to deal with failure than success.

I have a nervous sniff that I recognize when my son unconsciously mimics me. Forty years ago I went to Doctor Mann for a nervous tick in my eyes and a spastic twitch in my neck. They are symptoms of a roiling unhappy interior. As a kid, I kicked in neighborhood pumpkins, smashed Christmas lights, busted the windows out of garages. I heaved a hunk of ice through a stranger's front bay window. I got drunk on grain alcohol for the first time when I was twelve and many times since for numbing relief from my self-loathing and my unspoken anger.

I have chosen to be involved with chaotic or damaged

women. Melissa was not the cause of my downfall but rather an inevitability. I don't like Melissa, but if I'd married a sweet, passive woman, I might not have learned the truth about myself as soon as I did. I haven't had a strong voice other than the booming voice I found in fury. For most of my life, I have repaid perceived offenses with deceit and sometimes with self-righteousness and intimidation. Since my divorce, I have formed "safe" relationships with wounded women who need and adore me and are afraid that I'll leave them. This is not a combination for success.

When my children talk about their childhood, they remember me driving too fast, drunk, screaming at Melissa. To this day, they hate "All Things Considered" because that was the time of the day Melissa and I would start in on each other. Tony and Kay were drawn into our chaos feeling like they had to be our parents, and in so doing we robbed them of their childhood. They are still pissed.

The following is a list of offenses and abuses for which I hold you responsible:
Mother,

You did talk about my penis to my girlfriend and my wife.

You did crawl into my sleeping bag drunk then betrayed me to Dad for pinching you.

You have confided in me about your lack of sex with Dad for several decades.

The appearance of affairs with Benny Bradly and others, the suggestion that Stan the hairdresser was doing more than your hair, as a threat to Dad.

You slam the door shut with anger or disbelief when I am critical of you. I have been afraid to be openly critical of anyone for most of my life. Most recently on the phone you said you were in disbelief that I would bring this up again and that you had something in the oven so you had to go. This is typical of how you have handled my attempts at being critical of you.

You introduced me as your brother in a piano bar so you could get hit on.

During my teen years, your behavior was drunken and slutty. I watched you act flirty with my friend Dick.

You would burst into my room without knocking, to catch me naked, masturbating. I locked the door against you, and later on Melissa and I locked it for the same reason. I know Ben had a similar experience with you.

Dad,

You disappear from phone conversations in emotional moments, around anger, any situation that may require you to show up and be strong.

You want a clean version of the truth that wipes out any of my feelings.

You don't stand up for me. I wanted you to run interference between Mom and me. I tried to tell you in 1987, but you sided with Mom against me and told me it never happened. It did happen.

You have competed with me, covertly. I have been so afraid of open competition that I am covertly competitive even with my own son. I have successfully stunted his growth, too.

You are always more important to you than I am to you.

Your erotic magazines seemed to tell me that you weren't dealing with real women all that well. I followed your lead.

Much of this complaint is about childhood, but you haven't changed in how you deal with me to this day. You trash me or leave me when I am critical of you. Mother, please reread your letter to me after the last time I brought this up. You express no remorse for absolutely inexcusable behavior between a mother and son. Instead, you want to clean up your messy history by burying and burning the truth, denying that it happened. . . . This was your shit, not mine. . . . You should be ashamed, not me.

. . . My life would have been measurably different if you had sat me down hard and said: "This is my wife and I'll take care of her, Dean, you don't have to. One day you will grow up and have your own wife." I feel like I was required to be the pal to Mom that you weren't. I occupied her time. I vacuumed her living room floor and baked stuff for her approval. I remember her in tears, running from the dining room table. Somehow, I felt responsible.

. . . I have worked hard to get through the stumbling blocks to be able to be a good friend, mate, and father. I can take and give criticism. My self-righteousness is shrinking and my courage is growing. I can hear suggestions and accept offers of help. I really appreciate honesty in my friends. This sounds pathetic coming from a fifty year old man, but I have had to undo your legacy to me . . . I have come to like who I am. That won't change, but I find that I am still vulnerable to family poison around family reunions so I will be keeping my distance from you. I plan on being polite and friendly just not expecting anything from you any longer.

Dean

Dean is no longer engaged in the futile struggle that kept him angry and took such a toll on his life. He has stopped waiting for his parents to take him seriously before he takes himself seriously. He has stopped waiting for them to hold themselves responsible before he takes responsibility. Getting clear with parents often sets a healthy precedent. Dean wrote a letter to his girlfriend to begin the process of resolving feelings he had been unable to ex-

press to her. He followed up with a conversation. She was responsive in a way his parents were unable to be:

Carol,

    I know in my heart that I don't want to live the rest of my
life with you, and I bet you don't know that's how I feel. I don't
want to say good-bye. I want to clear this up with you. I can see
that my being romantic and attentive with you is probably
confusing to you. You and I are sweet to each other. The part
that's missing for me is a depth of intimacy. . . . I can't trust
that you know how you feel when you are angry, or scared, or
even what really makes you happy. I can't help you by being
your junior psychologist and I shouldn't be . . . trying to do
so. . . . I worry about the other guy rather than being able to
trust that they will take care of themselves so I can attend to
my own stuff. . . .

    I am being selfish by being vague about my long-term in-
tentions with you. By being vague, I get a lover, companion,
advisor, and friend. But will you be those for me if I remind
you that one day you and I will part? We went into this in-
tending to enjoy and investigate our attraction for one an-
other. . . . I feel like I am being deceitful and duplicitous
about where I am with you. I am not interested, right now, in
other women, so please don't go there with this. I don't want to
end what you and I do share, I just want to get clear with you.
With this said, you have to figure out where you are with me.

Dean

    It takes time to discover why a person is cut off from his feel-
ings, why he is unable to trust enough to love, and what it has to
do with his family relationships. In Ken's family, feelings were not
expressed, and if they were they were then denied or obliterated.

Ken wrote a series of letters to his parents trying to open up a dialogue, trying to express to them what he had never before expressed. (Ken's cover letter to his brother appeared in Chapter 7). Although Ken was more neglected than abused, the inability of his parents to deal with feelings, the emphasis on avoidance of conflict and cover-up, and the pressure to achieve at all costs helped hobble Ken. When he entered therapy, we saw a very bright, hyped-up young man who had made it in the business world, was earning huge amounts of money, but had no real friends, trusted no one, drank too much, was full of quick repartee, and constantly name-dropped. He was lonely, angry, and depressed and had no idea why:

1. Dear Mom,

I've spent some time recently trying to figure out why it is that I don't confront things that I need to confront. I can be in a situation that I dislike, I can know what I need to do to deal with it, but if admitting to how I'm feeling about the situation is required, I chicken out and don't act. . . . When I finally get miserable enough, I usually deal with the situation in a messy and frequently ugly way. I usually extract revenge at a later time and in an inappropriate way. For example, rather than confront Risa about her infidelity, I stayed in the relationship and made her increasingly miserable. When it finally ended, I delighted in shutting her out of my life.

. . . Why is it that I've been unable to address the feelings or hurt? I think I've figured it out. I keep remembering an incident from my childhood that I now believe to be important. It's one of many. . . .

I can remember being a little kid, living in the house that you hated on Highgate Road. I remember making a pot of popcorn and attempting to carry it somewhere. I grabbed the pot's

*handle too close to the pot. My fingers were wrapped around
the metal sleeve that connected the hot pot to the plastic handle. I got part of the way across the kitchen with the pot and
realized my fingers were burning. I panicked. I didn't want to
drop the hot pot on the linoleum floor because I knew it would
melt. The closest place I could set the pot was the dining room
table. I set the hot pot down on the bare table and started
screaming because my fingers hurt. I remember you coming to
the dining room to see what I was screaming about . . . and realizing that the tabletop was scorched. I remember you starting
to wail about the burned tabletop. . . . My finger was burned
and I felt badly because I realized that I'd done something bad
by putting that hot pot on the table. I wanted you to comfort
me. You kept wailing. I was frightened. I'd never heard you cry
like that. I didn't know what to do. I wanted you to stop. I ran
into my bedroom and got down on my knees and prayed to
God for you to stop. All I wanted to happen was for you to be
OK again.*

*I put my own hurt and feelings aside and focused on want-
ing you to be OK. . . . I've repeated this same scenario of
putting my feelings aside to placate the other party over and
over again since then, and I hate it. It makes me really angry
when I realize how lopsided my life has been as a result. I'm
working on being conscious of how I feel and being able to
deal with the feelings. . . . Being able to tell you how I felt on
that day so long ago is a sign of progress.*

K.

The response from Ken's parents was defensive and uncom-
prehending. It was not until an interaction with them on his
birthday that he made another effort to express his feelings. Ken
is clear about what is wrong by the time he writes in his second

letter, "We all keep trying to appear like everything is under control," and "I never learned how to fight or how to express any mad, bad, or sad feelings or anything that wasn't OK." He reaches out to his parents to try to get an exchange started in an effort to break up the polite nonrelationship he has had with them his whole life:

2. *Dear Mom and Dad,*

I'm writing this letter in order to help myself feel better. I expect that it will make you feel bad, but that is not its intent.

In lots of families, the parents try to make it easy for the kids. They arrange business introductions, assist with club memberships, provide advice and wisdom. . . . Somehow it feels like it's turned around for us. How can it be that you could visit me for my fortieth birthday and suggest that my employer pick up our dinner tab? How can it be that you let me pick up my own birthday dinner tab? How can it be that you'd consider asking me to use some of my liquid assets to tide you over . . . for your refinancing because you'd lose some money if you had to cash in a CD a few months early? It feels like I'm the parent here.

. . . I remember being told that, as the oldest, it was in part my responsibility to help care for my siblings. I remember not having orthodontia because we couldn't afford it, yet my sibs all had the chance. Now I'm forty and looking to finance it out of my own pocket. I chose Northeastern because you made it clear that the younger kids would need help with college expenses, too. So I worked summers, part time, and during school and got a job instead of going to graduate school. I paid most of my college expenses—including room and board myself. Lots of my acquaintances went to Europe and had other

adventures during their late teens and early twenties. I gener-
ated money so that there would be money to send the younger
kids to school. When Carl and Jake showed little interest in
college so that there were few college bills to pay, I felt even
more robbed. I developed a resentment of my siblings that I've
come to regret and have spent the last couple of years trying to
reduce the distance between us.

*   . . . It's not a surprise to me that when we do get together it*
feels awkward for me and probably for you. The time moves by
slowly, and it is a relief when the effort is over. Instead of feel-
ing good about your visit, instead of feeling loved or cared
about, I end up feeling damaged. It hurts to say this, but I'm
tired of pretending that it is otherwise.

*   You have almost no understanding of me, little understand-*
ing of the reasons I left my job, bought, and then sold the
house on Pine Drive, ever got married, ever got married to the
women I married, why I never had kids, and why I got di-
vorced. You were proud of me because I earned a lot, had a big,
visible job, and managed my money well . . . your enthusiasm
only shows when I'm talking about going to work and how
much I'll earn.

*   We all keep trying to appear like everything is under con-*
trol, like there's never any controversy or conflict. I can only re-
call two instances in my entire growing up when you two ever
fought. . . . I never learned how to fight or how to express any
mad, bad, or sad feelings. It always felt like impolite behavior.
I learned to appear like everything was always fine. Yet
everything was not always fine. And then I had no skills to do
anything about it.

*   Your bitterness about investment reversals, career disap-*
pointment, and other down points in your lives are kept hid-

den, not discussed until they leak out. I learned to always look in control and as a result, to this day, have an awfully hard time asking for help or taking it when it's offered. I still have a very difficult time expressing or admitting my real feelings about most things.

. . . I'm trying to understand how I feel and to communicate my feelings clearly to you. This is not my first effort. . . . I'll not give up without trying again.

I would love it if this letter results in us getting closer, but it doesn't appear to me that you want a real relationship with me or any of the family.

I hope you don't miss the point and focus on who paid for my birthday dinner like you focused on the Christmas gift that provided such a strong symbol for my last letter.

I've sent copies of this letter to Jake, Jane, and Carl. I hope it creates an opportunity for us all to address some of the issues I've raised. Please don't lose sight of the fact that I do love you. I just wish we were much closer than we are.

K.

P.S. Got your package. I think, if you read it again, you'll see that the poem talks about how parents sacrifice for their first-born. It doesn't talk about the firstborn except as a symbol for the parents' love for each other and sacrifice. I see nothing in it that expresses how proud you are of me. It's more self-congratulation than anything else. I appreciate your effort but . . . it's not about me. It's about you.

PPS. If you want to discuss this I want to do it by letter. I don't want to get into it over the phone.

The package Ken refers to was a poem his parents sent on Ken's fortieth birthday:

OUR FIRST CHILD

I've always loved you so because
You were our first miracle.
You were the genesis of a marriage
And the fulfillment of young love.
You sustained us through the hamburger years,
The first apartment (finished in early poverty)
And the 12 inch T.V. we paid for in 36 months.
You were new and had unused grandparents
And enough clothes for a set of triplets.
You were the original model for a mom & dad
Who were trying to work the bugs out.
You got the strained lamb, the open safety pins
And three hour naps.
You were the beginning.

AUTHOR UNKNOWN

By sending him a poem they thought they could convince him of their love and devotion. It was a cellophane-wrapped, cardboard-framed piece of "poetry" with little flowers by the title—the kind that you can pick up in a card store for a dollar or two. It came with a note signed by both parents. In the note his parents suggested that Ken needn't frame it and hang it unless he wished to, but they wanted him to know that it expressed their pride in their eldest and how much they loved him.

His parents' efforts to stop him from honestly expressing his feelings by sending him this "poem" was the turning point for Ken. As Ken continued to write his parents, he gradually understood that they were incapable of responding, and when he accepted that reality, he let go of his angry engagement with them.

In the past, when Ken no longer had his parents around to play out the old covertly negative script, he picked others to do the job. His two former wives, like his parents, had little skill in dealing with feelings and were afraid of their own emotions and of his. He perpetuated the situation he grew up in, re-creating the old script with new characters who, like his parents, were not bad people but so limited that they wanted the phony, puffed up, impressive "young Turk" Ken, not the real Ken. His wives, like his parents, not only could not help him be himself, they subtly pushed him to be hidden.

It is still a struggle for Ken to identify his feelings when he is hurt or angry. When he is feeling blue or insecure and is most in need of emotional contact, he still is likely to puff himself up by bragging or showing off, which further isolates him. But he knows this, and his friends do, too, and they can help him out of this old behavior by labeling it and telling him they are put off by it. Although it is hard for Ken to identify his feelings, once he does he is warm and open; he has gone from being stingy with himself and others to being generous. Ken continues to be in very limited but cordial contact with his parents.

10

Pacing the Letters

and Deciphering the Responses

After a victory at work, or when she felt close to someone, or when she had a breakthrough in her therapy group, Cindy would come so late to the next group that she would miss the work of the people she had felt close to the previous session. She would make sure she did not have time to talk about her good feelings or victories or do any therapy work. Even if there was time, she reasoned that she did not deserve to work because she had come so late. Her lateness and/or "disappearance" in group ensured that the other group members would get annoyed with her. She would leave the session feeling deprived and angry that the group members would not cut her some slack. Then when she was alone, she would obsessively criticize herself.

As a child, when Cindy revealed to her mother that she was happy or proud of herself, her mother, who was jealous of the attention her husband gave his daughter, told Cindy she was self-indulgent, prideful, and un-Christian to be happy when others were suffering. She criticized everything about Cindy, including her looks. Recently Cindy discovered a snapshot of herself as a little girl and was surprised to see that she had been very pretty.

By getting the group to be angry at her and then feeling self-critical, Cindy, like Lorna (Chapter 8), was controlling the anticipated bad response that always followed the expression of positive feelings in her family.

When Cindy had negative or critical feelings, she employed a different coping strategy; she denied her feelings and perceptions (in her words, she "forgot" her feelings). Cindy had learned by example to dissociate from the bad things she saw or heard: Her mother denied her father's drunken and/or inappropriately sexual behavior, and her mother, father, and brother denied her perceptions when she spoke out. She learned to do to herself what her parents had done, deny her reality. When Cindy is angry or hurt she (often automatically) "forgets" her feelings and then acts them out.

Being openly critical or angry or hurt was so negatively reinforced in Cindy's family (as was being openly proud or happy) that it was an adaptive solution to dissociate from these feelings and act them out passively. Unlike Dr. B., who was always aware of the bad things that went on in her family, Cindy became fully aware of the emotional abuse, the secrets, and the hypocrisy in her family only after she had been in therapy many years. Even then her first instinct was to deny and protect her parents. She vigorously defended her father against her critical feelings and thoughts because he was the only one in the family who gave her any positive response, contaminated and sexualized though it often was. Cindy can still be bought off, at least temporarily, with the slightest acknowledgment from her parents, boss, boyfriend, or friends. She is often willing to think the best, even while she is feeling angry.

A great benefit of letter writing is that the writer has tangible documents (her own letter[s] and the response[s] to it) that she can refer back to as often as she wants. She can decipher and analyze these documents in her own time. She may ask her allies to help her when she gets stuck.

Cindy wrote a series of letters to her parents over a period of three years. I include them in chronological order. Her letters illustrate the importance of pacing confrontation. She took advantage of her therapy group to help her decipher her parents' responses and her responses to their responses. Only after deciding that she thoroughly understood the subject she was addressing, felt comfortable expressing her feelings about her parents related to that topic, and (in those instances when she received a response) had analyzed her parents' response letter, did she write a confrontational letter home. This pacing is especially important for those who, like Cindy, use dissociation as a major defense against pain, because as they write they uncover more and more events along with the feelings attached to these events. The writing process helps the writer reclaim experiences and feelings that she has previously walled off from her awareness.

Each of Cindy's letters elicited a response that paralleled the responses she got growing up when she dared to tell her parents what she honestly felt or thought. The fact that many of the bad experiences of the past were re-created in response to her present attempts to communicate gave Cindy a reality test that broke through her continued efforts to deny a particularly painful reality by putting herself down. In between letters, she would start to deny her perceptions and feel bad about herself, but she had the concrete document of a letter or sometimes a tape of her parents' phone call to help her figure out what was really going on. This helped her peel away the layers to get to the core truth about herself and her family:

1. Dear Mom and Dad,

I got the subscription to Guideposts. . . . *This is a gift that makes you feel good about yourself—but it's not something I want, and you know it. I don't think you see me at all. My interests and talents are totally overlooked because all you're thinking about is whether I'm going to church.*

Christmas day is the same. You're not interested in me— you're worried about people at church that you're taking care of. . . . I can't enjoy getting or giving presents because of all the guilt you pass on—"we shouldn't get presents—we don't really need them," "other people need them more," "Christmas isn't really about presents, it's religious." You take all the happiness out of gift-giving. It's so nice to visit friends and not have all the judgment and "shoulds" attached to Christmas.

The other reason I don't like Christmas with you is because seeing you both reminds me of all the years when my father was drinking and my mother didn't want to deal with him so made him go and sleep in my room. I was miserable but had to act like everything was fine. . . .

All of this (and more—I can elaborate sometime, if you are interested) is why I've decided that I'm not coming home for Christmas. I'm going to spend it with friends.

Cindy

P.S. I'm canceling the Guideposts *subscription.*

In this first letter Cindy has an annoyed but measured tone. She uses the topic of Christmas to organize some of her feelings and thoughts about the past and present. Cindy's letters progress incrementally in scope of material and in level of confrontation. Notice that she periodically refers to her parents in a way that provides her distance from them; she writes, "my father" or "my mother." As the series progresses, this drops out:

2. *Dear Mom and Dad,*

I got your card a few weeks ago (and the letter before that). You think I just need to hear how much you love me—if you say it enough, I'll get over this and come home, like the prodigal child.

That's not what's going on.

I stay away because "home" was not a good home for me. . . . After I talked with you at New Year's, you both said you wished I had talked before about my unhappiness. I knew if I told you, you wouldn't listen to my feelings and you'd blame me, tell me I was at fault or that I shouldn't feel that way because it wasn't Christian. How many times have I said something hurt my feelings and was told, "You're being too sensitive"? Growing up, I was often labeled as "sensitive," as "getting my feelings easily hurt"—so I learned to blame myself (and to never be angry at people who were taking advantage of me or abusing me) and to pretend I was happy when I wasn't.

You said in the letter in May that you want to get this resolved so we can get back to the "good times." For me, those "good times" were not good—I was depressed and lonely and had no self-esteem.

You know what I remember? I remember my mother pointing out, over and over, that my mouth was too big ("like Martha Raye's"), my nose was too big, my face too long. Then my father started in—calling me "crip" when I had chorea and couldn't walk much, and "four-eyes" when I got glasses, and "big bruiser" when I gained weight from being sick. Then when I was eleven and started to develop breasts, my father used to embarrass me by pointing at my chest and saying,

"What's that?" The times that either of you complimented me, told me I was pretty . . . were rare. My mother was the most important one to give me feelings about my looks, about being a girl—and she was picking me apart, making me feel ugly. And the most important man in my life, my father, did the same thing. How could I feel attractive and expect men to find me appealing after this?

Mom, I was closer to Dad growing up . . . you criticized me, saying I was "Daddy's girl" and that I looked like his side of the family, and then pointed out faults with the Powells and how they looked. You'd say all these things in a "nice" way so they didn't sound so mean . . . you talked about how my brother looked like the Spandler side of the family and made them (and him) sound prettier. It was you and my brother on one side and me and Daddy on the other. . . . I look back at pictures of myself at six or seven—I was so pretty. Why didn't you acknowledge this?

The same thing happened with school. I loved to read, but was constantly criticized and called "lazy" because I had my "nose in a book." I was in advanced classes all through school and should have been hearing encouragement, which would have given me confidence. I started college feeling ugly, not smart, aware of all my imperfections, and not at all aware of my abilities and good qualities. I was shocked to find out that other people saw me as smart and responsible. . . . You didn't want me to give up the boring, dead end job I had in the university bookstore. Whenever I talked about going back to school, you'd start lamenting the fact that I'd be "giving up good benefits" and the "security of a permanent job with the state." You encouraged Peter to get a master's degree in economics—why didn't you do the same for me?

The only reason I have a great job now is because I went

back to school, with no financial or moral support from either of you. The whole time I was in graduate school, Dad kept saying, "Hurry up and get out and get a job." Last year, Mom, when you came to visit a friend and to meet me for lunch, I told your friend I wanted to learn more. You laughed and shook your head in an embarrassed, disapproving way and said, "She's one of those permanent students." I was astonished. First, because it wasn't true. I'd finished school ten years earlier. Second, because you were disapproving of my wanting to keep learning. And third, because you implied I was not doing anything, which was absurd since I've worked since I was eight. If I ever acted like I didn't want to work weekends and summers in the factory, you'd tell me how lazy I was. I've worked two jobs ever since I can remember. . . . In graduate school . . . I was working four nights a week in restaurants. . . . You sent money to charities, church—and, in the meantime, I was living in a house overrun with rats. (Dick used to say, "You're living like a refugee" and couldn't understand why you weren't helping me.) . . . It's as if I were an orphan and, instead of helping me, your daughter, you were sending money to another orphanage.

Do you know what I do in my job now? I get called as a consultant to go to all different areas of the hospital to assess patients with both psychiatric and alcohol/drug problems—and to train doctors in how to treat them. . . . It's a good thing I didn't listen to you.

I remember mother talking obsessively about illnesses and diseases. Always harping on how we were going to get sick, or how Dad was going to have a heart attack, or asking handicapped people all about the details of their injury. When I think of growing up, I hear mother either predicting that someone's going to get sick, or saying that someone has just

learned they have an illness, or all about someone's death. . . .
I was amazed to start working in a hospital and to learn that
people there don't talk about illnesses very much, unless they
have to.

This left me constantly thinking something terrible was go-
ing to happen, just when things were going well—a disaster
was around every corner. . . . I'm not sure what the point of all
this was, other than to keep me home, afraid to do anything,
scared of the world, worried. And depressed.

But the very thing you should have been worrying over, you
pretended was not a problem. It horrifies me that you think
Dad wasn't "too" bad when he drank—you thought it was OK
because he was a "nice" drunk, not a mean one. You left me
alone with him. I had to listen while he poured out his heart
and got weepy. All evening, he'd go back and forth to the bath-
room to drink bourbon from the bottle he kept in his drawer. I
couldn't figure out what was wrong with me, *why I didn't*
want to listen to him. Everyone kept telling me, "Mr. Powell is
a wonderful man," so I convinced myself they were right and I
was wrong. One night he got sick and kept throwing up in the
bathroom. I thought he was dying. I finally called Mom at
work and she said, "Oh, he just had a little too much to drink."

Mom, you minimized what was going on and you're still do-
ing it. The truth is, you liked it when he drank. You thought
the sappy, sentimental mush he was saying was true and you
wanted to hear it. You wanted him *to get drunk because then*
he'd start saying how much you meant to him. I remember you
telling me that when he was drinking he'd tell you what was
really on his mind, tell you all the feelings he normally
couldn't talk about, would let you know how much he loved
you. You encouraged him to drink, never considering what it
was like for me. . . . I finally said something to Dad about his

drinking when I was in college—and he was surprised that I knew he drank. He said something like, "Oh, you weren't supposed to know." . . . You pretended you could do whatever you wanted in front of me. You acted like I was an idiot who couldn't see all this. . . . Neither of you talked about the drinking, and the silence made it worse. I had this ugly secret and doubted what I was seeing and feeling because everyone was telling me I was too critical, too sensitive. I learned to walk around blind to people's faults, ignoring them when they were mean to me because I thought it was my fault. I had to think only good things about people and never criticize them.

What resulted from all this? I married Rusty, an alcoholic and a tyrant. I'd learned about keeping secrets so I didn't tell you any of this at the time. He used to get very upset, throw tantrums, tell me, "If you love me, you won't do this . . ." in order to get me to stay home with him. . . . He'd plead that he wouldn't be able to sleep if I went out alone because he'd be so worried. I thought I must be really selfish to want to go out when it upset him and gave in. He wouldn't let me drive anywhere alone for two years and I put up with it. . . . I wasted years in a miserable marriage, which was more like prison. I was depressed and starting to feel suicidal when I finally found a therapist who helped me gain some confidence and self-esteem.

. . . It's not enough to say, "It's in the past and God's forgiven it," and it won't work to put a "smiley face" on it and wish it away. That is part of the problem. Whenever I said how bad something was, you'd tell me in various ways not to be so negative or critical, to forgive, to be "Christian" toward people who hurt me. You left me no room to be angry when people abused me. When I was excited or proud, you'd tell me I shouldn't

brag on myself, or let it "go to my head"—so I couldn't feel good about myself without feeling guilty. . . .

I'm not going to continue to act like things weren't so bad— it was bad and it's still affecting my life in bad ways. Two times in the past, I talked to Dad about things that bothered me, and each time he had a heart attack a week later. What a way to make me feel guilty—like I was upsetting him so much, he might even die. . . . All my life, I felt like I couldn't say what bothered me because you'd both be so hurt and devastated. So don't blame me for not telling you all of this before. You taught me it was not all right to talk about my true feelings. Blaming me (and getting me to believe I was at fault) was the way you kept me from criticizing you. If that trick still worked, I would have read your letter, felt like I was at fault because I should have told you all this before, and stopped saying what I need to say. . . .

Dad, what's really incredible is that you were being so judgmental after having an affair with Nellie Burton. You said Mom knows all about this—does she know you used to get me to go with you for truck rides at night so you could drive by Nellie's house? You acted like I was deaf and dumb. How could you involve me in your deception? Then you had me work with Nellie that summer, in the factory. I knew this secret and was caught right in the middle. Nellie would keep trying to find out about you and our family. You made me a guilty party to all this—you can't imagine how it made me feel to be around my mother, wondering if she knew about it.

I've never understood why you'd involve me in all this, but now it seems clear. You were getting something out of being sexual and showing off in front of me. The same way you used to like to sit around exposing yourself in your boxer shorts all the time (but then jumping all over Dick for showing up at the dinner table without a shirt!) . . . And insist on hugging all of my girlfriends when they came over. And telling me when I was in a bathing suit that you were born "twenty years too late." . . . You were enjoying all this sexy showing off in front of me, and Mom didn't stop you. She'd come home at night, walk into the den where we were watching TV, and see you sitting there with your shorts open and everything showing and say, "James, shame on you," and walk over and close your shorts. This happened night after night. Mom would be coy, flirting, making sex jokes too. And to sleep in my room when you were drinking—it makes me wonder why you did that, if anything else happened that I can't remember? . . . Mom, you said some pretty bad things happened to you growing up. I'm upset that you had those painful experiences and still allowed similar things to happen to me.

For years, you've both judged me, preached at me, measured me (and others) by whether we're "saved." After Rusty left Divinity School and his church internship, Dad told me, "You were on the road to Heaven and you got off of it." And behind all this preaching, and making me feel guilty because I wasn't good enough and was "sinning" (by not going to church, by not being in Bible studies, by living with Dick) was an appalling amount of hypocrisy. Lying to me, committing adultery and involving me in it, getting drunk. . . . And then, instead of helping me, you've stood by and watched me struggle. You both retired at fifty-five, traveled all over the world while I was working to get through school. You gave money to PTL and charities and never offered to help me. I think you owe it to me now to pay the $8,500 I scraped up for school . . . I doubt that you will be able to understand or take responsibility for the

emotional damage. But you can and should make up for some
of it by paying for it. . . .

If you want to write, then please don't send those sappy mes-
sages about how wonderful I am and how everyone misses me,
etc. That's not responding and it ignores the anger I feel.

Cindy

By the time Cindy wrote this letter, she was well aware that she had problems ignoring her own feelings and she understood how and why she learned to do this. Cindy's mother wrote a letter in return and signed for both parents. In sum, she asked for forgiveness for what Cindy "said" they did. She went on to explain that the past is past and to say how hard things had been for her and her husband growing up. She said that Cindy was always too sensitive. She implied that if Cindy could not immediately forgive them and concentrate on the good in the family now that they had said they were sorry, Cindy was a bad person.

Before Cindy could reply, she needed to decipher the covert messages in her parents' letter. At first she was confused by the seeming apology. She thought that she should be feeling grateful that they asked for forgiveness, but she felt guilty, angry, and put down. Her group encouraged her to analyze the response letter so that she could identify and decipher the covert messages as well as the overt ones. After this exercise, Cindy realized how powerfully discombobulating her parents' defensive responses were to her and how it was that she lost ground in the past whenever she tried to express her viewpoint. She had learned in her family to give up the attempt to express herself or to even pay attention to her feelings because she always ended up feeling worse, guilty and mean-spirited for making her parents uncomfortable or upset and neurotically oversensitive for taking seriously what they maintained were just jokes or not intentional. Because Cindy now had their responses in black and white, she could take as much time as she needed to regain her equilibrium before she responded.

It is not uncommon that a physical or emotional abuser will ask for forgiveness in one sentence and then in the same or next sentence play victim or blame the letter writer. In the past, when Cindy tried to talk about anything controversial, her parents' mixed messages so confused and stymied her that she felt only impotent rage and sadness. But when a confronting letter is sent and the response is in letter form, it is easier to decipher the mixed messages. Messages that discombobulate a writer in face-to-face interaction can become a teaching document when they appear in a letter. This document can be revisited and diagrammed so that the overt and covert messages can be deciphered with help from others who either did not grow up with mixed messages and can recognize them more easily or who grew up with mixed messages and learned how to decipher them.

Sometimes a client will bring into her therapy group a response letter that she thinks is a fairly good response, but somehow the letter leaves her feeling upset. When the group reads the response letter, they are baffled that she thinks the letter is okay. The group members are reading both the overt and covert messages. The receiver, like Cindy at the start of her letter therapy, has not yet learned this skill. All she "gets" is the overt message, but she "feels" the covert messages. As in the past, the covert messages have bypassed her thinking. Remember Cindy's parents responded with "I'm sorry that you *feel* we treated you this way" or "I'm sorry for what you *say* we did." At first the letter writer fails to pay attention to the retraction embedded in the words "feel" and "say" that immediately follow the "I'm sorry." The best way to teach the writer is to use the response letter. Once the writer learns to decipher her parents' messages in a letter, she can bring this skill to any communication or interaction.

In addition to learning these deciphering skills, the mere process of writing successive letters and rereading the letters and the responses to them engenders the recall and integration of feelings with specific events. Once these feelings and events are integrated, the writer can face her parent with increased clarity of thought. Cindy's third letter includes more material to illustrate her points and explain her feelings:

3. *Dear Mom and Dad,*

I received your letter. . . . At no point do you acknowledge your faults. Once again, you've turned it back on me, saying I'm too sensitive, that I "interpreted things out of context," that Dad was only "joking." You make it clear that you don't believe what I say—"We can only ask forgiveness for everything that you say that we did," as if I made up what happened.

This is exactly the way you acted when I was growing up. But I have had some hope that you'd both listen and practice some of the things you preach.

. . . What I left out of the first letter were a number of incidents when I was a teenager. The biggest one was the affair Dad and Aunt Ginny had. Recently, I've let myself remember the number of times I was standing in the kitchen with Mom and Uncle Bob, watching Aunt Ginny getting more and more drunk and hugging and falling over Dad. The two of them would disappear down the hall to Dad's bedroom where he kept the bourbon. . . . Mom, you and your brother would watch all of this and cook dinner . . . and act nice and sweet . . . both of you were pretending nothing sexual was going on . . . I couldn't believe you would both put up with this. . . .

My life has been a wasteland of sadness, isolation, and empti-ness. I could not let myself feel because then I would have to go through this anger and hurt. I have . . . only recently been able to recognize when men are being abusive to me. . . . No wonder Dad always liked Jimmy Swaggart so much—he acts just like him (including the phony crying and asking for for-giveness when he gets caught having sex with someone).

The second thing I omitted was from your anniversary a few years ago. Mom started retelling the story about how she and Dad met in Brooklyn when he was in the Navy. You decided on the spur of the moment to get married. Mom, you told us how you were dressed and waiting for Dad. And you waited and waited. His Navy buddies showed up and you began to think he wasn't coming so his friends went to look for him. I can't re-call if they found him and brought him along or if he just showed up, but I remember you saying he was unshaved, di-sheveled, and smelled of alcohol . . . what a disappointment your wedding must have been. . . .

You said Dad told you his Navy buddies had played a "mean practical joke" on him: they got a jar of "crabs" and threw them on him and then he gave you crabs on your honeymoon. And then you laughed. . . . He got crabs because he had sex with some other woman before you got married and that's the only way he could have gotten crabs. . . . Dad made a total fool of you. . . . All the signs were there that he was going to screw around on you and you just didn't want to see it, even when he did it right in front of you.

What a picture to present to a little girl of how you let men treat you. A man shows up for his wedding dirty, late, drunk the night before, gives you crabs on your honeymoon—no wonder I settled for so little in men and let them abuse my feelings. . . . I remember being sixteen and at the beach and Dad got drunk and went on a ride with Janet where they were standing in a cage facing each other and when the ride would swing up and down, I was mortified to see him rubbing up against her.

I used to be so uncomfortable and uneasy about being alone with Dad and this is probably why . . . sitting around in his underwear exposing himself, hugging me in a sexual way. . . . I was a target for Dad's sexual advances. And so were other girls. And women. It happened all the time and I tried not to remember it. Mom, you did the same and so didn't protect me. You even pushed him my way because you were avoiding sex. . . . It's time you stop hiding behind religion and own up to this.

Cindy

Cindy had confronted her mother with potent material that her mother had denied in the past. Not surprisingly, Cindy's mother wrote an angry defensive letter in response. At this point in the letter series, Cindy gave up hope because her mother's letter revealed that she was unwilling (unable?) to make any effort to move beyond her fury to try to understand what her daughter was feeling. In her next letter Cindy reiterates what she has said, tells her parents why she is giving up on them, and tries to balance the picture realistically by including what she appreciates about them as a way of saying good-bye. This letter is an attempt to break the futile and destructive contact she has had with them:

4. Dear Mom and Dad,

When I started writing you a year ago, I had some hope that you'd both be able to respond in a way that would make it possible to resolve some of what happened when I was growing up. . . . Not only have you both shown no understanding for the ways you . . . ignored my feelings and blamed me when you were at fault, you've refused to admit that you did anything wrong. . . . You've decided that I'm exaggerating and lying and are once again blaming me.

This is exactly what happened to me as a child—and you're doing it again. For me to continue trying to talk to you is to continue this pattern. . . .

The one thing I have learned from this is that I don't have to be friends with people who are mean to me. I don't have to stay and try to talk to them, I can just leave—and find friends who are considerate and loving. With no help from you, and really in spite of you, I have been able to overcome the low self-esteem and problems from growing up.

I have had to learn to hear criticisms of how I ignored people's feelings (this is what you don't seem to be able to do), to be honest with friends and coworkers, and to pick men who are worthy of me. It's been very hard work, but I feel good about myself now, am happy, and have some very close friends. (I'm doing well at work, too.) Over a hundred people applied for a new job here, and I'm one of the two finalists.

I do have a few good memories of you both. Mom, I remember how much you like to play and to jitterbug and dance. And even though you hated the beach, we were finally able to get you to come out and play with us in the water and you were fun—you used to laugh and giggle a lot. I've learned to be this way and I'm glad you passed this on to me. And Dad, you used to love to play, too. You used to stay in the water swimming at the beach and ride rides with us and take me to ball games. I liked watching basketball games with you both. And you taught me to take vacations and to be adventuresome. I've kept this—and have become a good sailor and really enjoy playing.

It makes me sad that you can't change how you act toward

me. I didn't deserve what happened in my childhood, and I deserve much more now.

So it's time for me to stop. You've both said how happy you've been the past few years, and I hope that continues for you.

Cindy

Her parents used the positive comments in Cindy's letter to deny all that Cindy had previously written. They assumed that everything was okay again. They immediately called her and said as much. This next letter is a response to their phone call:

5. Dear Mom and Dad,

You missed the point of the letter, which was to say "goodbye" to both of you. I've accepted the sad truth that my parents made my childhood lonely, painful, and depressing—and that they'll never understand. . . . If you had been able to, we might have been able to have a relationship—but you've continued to blame me and excuse yourselves. . . .

I believe if you reread my letter, you'll see there's nothing in it indicating I want to talk to you or see you.

Cindy

Cindy was furious that her parents thought they could use her few positive comments to get her to drop all her complaints and go back to denying the past and her feelings about them, so that they could feel like good parents. This time her anger and her clarity about her parents' responses helped her complete the process of giving up hope and disentangling herself. She made a decision that since she could not get understanding or acknowledgment from her parents, all that she could get would be money to help pay the price of undoing the damage. With this in mind she wrote a letter requesting reimbursement for therapy costs.

A sequence of letters followed. Cindy received an impersonal birthday card with an imprinted "We love you." Next came a letter from her parents' lawyer saying that her memories are real to her and that her parents may pay her therapy costs out of love for her, but they would want assurances that she would not insist on more money to pay for future therapy. They requested a meeting with Cindy in a session with a therapist. Cindy responded through her lawyer that her past treatment expenses are all she will ask for and that after she received the money she would be open to meeting with them in a joint therapy session.

When Cindy did not hear from her parents after she had responded to their lawyer's letter, she called home and talked to her mother. In the conversation, which Cindy taped, her mother claimed that they never actually said that they would pay her therapy bills. At one point her mother denied her father's alcoholism altogether. Cindy said he got drunk every Monday and Friday. Her mother quickly corrected her and said no, it was every Tuesday and Thursday. In the conversation, her mother tried to deny that her father had affairs, although in a letter to Cindy both her father and mother had claimed that he had admitted his affairs to his wife and that they had both put such matters behind them. For the first time, Cindy responded to her mother's denial of facts and events calmly and logically. It helped that she had her parents' documented admissions. Cindy was genuinely surprised when she realized that her mother became rattled and lied when Cindy stood firm. When she told her group about the phone conversation, she knew that it was the first time in her life that she had completely held her ground with her mother; throughout the conversation she had been thinking clearly and expressing herself directly and spontaneously. She did not feel the impotent rage she had felt in the past. Her straight-from-the-heart letters and her unhurried analysis of her parents' letters to her prepared her for the telephone conversation with her mother. Her group cheered her victory.

Cindy understands that no matter what her parents do from now on, she no longer believes that they have to acknowledge her feelings and perceptions in order for her to be all right. Although she clearly would like to have her parents pay her past education or therapy costs and to have some joint counseling to deal with the impasse they are at with her, she has overcome her parents as obstacles to the rest of her life. She finally feels free and powerful. Cindy knows that this is more important than money or revenge. Listening to the tape of the telephone conversation with her mother, she could judge how far she had come.

We use whatever tools we get to survive. A phrase Cindy remembers hearing in church and from her fundamentalist parents was "Lean not unto thine own understanding" (Proverbs 3:5–7). In Cindy's family, this message from the Old Testament and Saint Paul was roughly translated as "Do not feel what you feel or know what you know. Feel and know only what (the Lord says) you ought to feel or know." This message was used to control and manipulate Cindy, to try to get her to mirror her parents' beliefs. Cindy used this phrase to help her dissociate from her despair and rage, from her awareness of the difference between the outward do-good Christian atmosphere of her home and the venal underbelly, with its secrets, lies, and deceit. She learned that what she saw and heard, witnessed and felt, was to be ignored and kept secret. The party line was the accepted reality.

Cindy did not become crazy; she adapted by hiding her real feelings and using Biblical phrases as mantras to anesthetize herself from the pain of those real feelings. It was only when she started writing letters that she (and for that matter I) became aware that she dissociated (completely blocking herself from her feelings) when she felt angry, critical, or hurt and that she used

Saint Paul's teachings and certain phrases from the Old Testament to help her dissociate.[1]

All the insight in the world could not change her destructive pattern until she confronted her parents and observed their response in a way that was open and verifiable. Each of her letters brought defensive and attacking responses from her family. At first, in spite of her requests, her parents refused to write and called instead. Cindy always taped the phone conversations and always went over the tapes in the way she would have gone over written responses.

Facing what she knew about her past and confronting her parents enabled Cindy to understand that she dissociates, to know why, and to anticipate when. She is starting to reverse the pattern—to feel the feelings and air her criticisms. She has found that not everyone will deny responsibility and blame her and that her good critical brain is an asset, not a liability. Cindy now understands that it is good to know what she knows and feel what she feels.

As Cindy disconnects from her family and her hopes that they will understand and accept her, she is quick to identify and avoid people who are like her family. She is more able to decipher the covert messages she gets and to be assertive on her own behalf. Cindy is clearly better off with the reality of no family than the myth of a positive family. But it is very hard for her, especially since she has no new family (except for her group) to replace the old toxic one.

It is probable that Cindy will never know what happened in her bedroom the nights she was left with her drunken father. I believe it is not essential for her therapy that she remembers whether she was an incest victim. She does not need to have knowledge of everything that happened to her. It is enough for her recovery and health that she has the general picture of the behavior in her family: the hypocrisy, the use of fundamentalist Christianity to cover up and control behavior, the rigidity and lack of openness and honesty, and the total disregard for feelings.

Many neuroscientists maintain that because of the way the brain develops, it is physically impossible to remember abuse that occurs before the age of three to three and a half. So there is much that cannot be accurately remembered no matter how competent and responsible the client and no matter how competent and responsible the therapist.[2]

As a result of composing and sending her letters and dealing with the responses they elicited, Cindy knows that her mother allowed bad things to happen to her, especially as they related to her father. Cindy knows that she did the same by allowing her alcoholic husband to mistreat her.

I think there is some serious sidetracking in the current debate in the literature and news media concerning the validity of memories of abuse.[3] I do not believe in excavating memories by hypnosis or any other artificial means because these methods fail to follow the natural pacing and unfolding process, which is important to insight and change. Although a bad therapist may be able to encourage a particularly hysterical or compliant client to believe something happened that did not, a good therapist may in the natural course of therapy be able to uncover a client's denial about family pathology that then enables the client to take responsibility for the present and let go of what responsibility she may have taken for her parents' pathology.[4]

All the uproar about memories and the possibility of memory distortion and even false memories becomes less problematic if there is a written dialogue in the present. If the recipient of the letter is defensive and, at the same time, fails to dispute specific accusations, events, or experiences, the letter dialogue will make it clear that the writer is bringing up a reality that the recipient wants to obliterate.

Over and over in their responses to her letters, Cindy's parents do not deny what happened. Instead, they try very hard to minimize the consequences of their actions and assert how Cindy was oversensitive or treating *them* harshly and unfairly by dredging up the past. For example, her father told Cindy in a conversation after the second letter that she should not "crucify him with the past." Neither parent refuted any of Cindy's accusations in a letter or in conversation except when Cindy threatened exposure and asked for reimbursement. Then her mother denied what she had never before disputed.

One of the values of getting a written dialogue going, even if the letter writers seem to be butting heads, is that it provides evidence. In her third letter, Cindy wrote her parents that anytime she voiced critical or negative feelings or perceptions they said she was being too sensitive—that is, it was her problem. In this way, she wrote, they controlled her and stopped her from sharing her feelings. After receiving this letter her mother responded, "As you say, you always were so sensitive." This reply enraged Cindy, but when she calmed down she saw that here was proof of her perceptions in black and white—evidence that her memory was correct. She will not forget experiences she had with them in the past because they are repeated in the present.

A Confrontational Letter

STEP BY STEP

Alex, who was just out of college at the time and not a therapy client, is a friend of my younger son Brandon. Alex came to live with us for a few months to get away from home before he and Brandon went to live in Argentina between college and graduate school. Living at home, he said, was getting him down. While Alex was with us, I was writing *Letters Home*. He asked about my book and after a number of discussions about the underlying principles of letter therapy, he decided to write a letter to his family and extended family in the hopes that he would feel better. He wanted Brandon and me to critique it, and he wanted specific guidelines on how to write his first draft.

I told Alex it is important to hold nothing back in the first draft. He should think of this draft as his chance to say everything he always wanted to say but was afraid to express. A good way to start is to focus on the predominant feelings you associate with the significant person(s) you are going to write to. In Alex's case, he felt angry, alienated, sad, and depressed, and he had a strong desire to change the family dynamics.

It is essential to pinpoint specific interactions you have had with the person to whom you are writing to illustrate your strongest feelings. Often these incidents are the ones the writer cannot keep out of his mind. He keeps going over and over them, and each time he does he feels the same bad feelings he felt when the incident first happened. It is particularly important to write down those incidents that have been kept secret and that you still feel pressured to keep secret. It is helpful to explain how you feel about having kept the secret all this time and how it makes you feel to be writing about it now.

Include what you/they have missed because you were not being real and open with your feelings before. Tell them why you have decided to be honest now. Be sure to explain (often it is good to start with this) what motivates you to write so openly now. Tell the person(s) you are writing to what you expect this letter will do for you and for your relationship with them if you get a receptive, open response, and what good it will do even if you get no response or a defensive, negative one.

Give instructions about what you want to happen in response to your letter. Do you want them (if there is more than one) to write separate letters? Do you want them to call? Do you want to ask them to try not to be defensive? Do you want to predict what response you are afraid they will give and ask them to resist that and give instead serious consideration to what you have said? Do you want them to first say what they agree with and only afterward what they disagree with or contest?

Part way through his first draft, Alex reported that thoughts and feelings were pouring onto the page, but that the more he said the more worried he became that he would hurt everyone's feelings. I told him that was probably true, but when he was not honest he ended up acting out his feelings by becoming sullen, depressed, avoiding his family, or being hostile to them or by becoming self-destructive. I said that I thought he was naive to think that these behaviors did not hurt him and them in the long run more than his honesty would. I agreed with him that his letter would probably not receive a welcome reception; it would very likely upset everyone in his family to know what he really felt and how critical he was of the entire family. They would probably get defensive and it would certainly get worse before it got better. I also told him I thought that he would feel better right away if he expressed all his feelings in the letter, even if he never sent it. At this point I remembered to tell him about the "take-aways" many of my clients had used to make their letters less powerful, such as minimizing or using psychobabble. He smiled and said that he had used many of these but would rewrite to try to eliminate them.

Alex began to worry that his letter was starting to sound as if he didn't love his family. He told me he wanted to write about the good things, and that was confusing him. This is a common worry, especially for someone in a well-meaning family. The solution is to separate the negative confrontation from the appreciations. In fact, it is often the hidden anger and the secrets that have gotten in the way of love and appreciation. Expressed positive feelings are contaminated by unexpressed negative feelings.

It is important to remember that a letter that is intended to be critical is not a letter of appreciation. In the letter home, the negatives need to be separated from the positives. I encourage the writer to put the positives that emerge on a separate sheet so they do not get mixed in with the negatives and prevent the writer from finally saying what he needs to say. I advised Alex to mention his positive feelings only in the context of his motivation for communicating freely about those feelings that get in the way of intimacy with his family.

Alex came up against another common barrier when he began to recognize that he had behaved in the family in ways that he felt ashamed of and regretted. I advised Alex not to wait to write the letter until he felt blameless because he would have to wait forever. I explained that his new sense of the truth's complexity was a very important byproduct of the draft process of the letter home. A closer approximation to the whole truth emerges. It is hard to stay self-righteous with "them" as the total bad guys and you as the total good guy if you are serious about writing an honest letter.

Equally as important as getting to this new truth is not using your new awareness of your contribution to stop you in your tracks. If we grow up thinking we have a right to express our negative critical feelings only if we are totally blameless, we either remain mute or delude ourselves that we are completely in the right. When the writer moves away from self-righteous rage and sees his contribution to the problems, I suggest that he keep that awareness for his own growth and for later exchanges between him and the parent—but not mix it in with his confrontation. The first critical letter home is not the place to elaborate on your sins lest this give those you are confronting a chance to dismiss you and bolster their defenses and you a chance once again to avoid expressing difficult feelings.

Writing home, like other writing, is ineffective if it is not clear. It is important not to go for subtlety. The language should be plain so that nothing stands between the writer and the reader. When the letter writer gets too literary or baroque, I tell him to write the way he would talk if he were a smart ten-year-old.

Alex's first draft was excellent. The main feedback I gave him was that his dramatic curses at the world in general hid his real feelings toward particular family members and distracted the reader from the point he was making. Though the swearing at the universe was peculiar to Alex (I think it may be age-related: Alex is significantly younger than most of my clients), the effort not to point to anyone in particular when you are internally blaming a particular person is very common. We are raised to believe that it is not polite or productive to blame the other person even if this is what we really think and feel. Therapists often further this notion by admonishing clients not to blame. Some therapists even go as far as teaching their clients to use contorted English: "You make me angry when you ignore me" gets transformed to more "PC" language: "I make myself angry when you ignore me." This creates crooked interactions and communication; the other person feels blamed anyway but cannot respond directly to the accusation because it has not been made directly. If you hold someone responsible, it saves a lot of time and energy to tell her directly. Even if it makes her more defensive initially, it immediately gets to the bottom of the conflict and therefore quickens a resolution.

After our discussion, Alex forced himself to pinpoint his feelings toward particular family members. He clarified examples that either Brandon or I found unclear. Although he had edited out the obvious take-aways, a few subtle take-aways remained. He eliminated these. He cut some irrelevant and/or repetitive writing. In places where he had implied what he felt, Brandon and I asked him to explain to us what he really felt; he then spelled this out in his letter. He made revisions easily and was proud of the finished product.

Although Alex was afraid of the response he would get, he felt relieved, brave, and cheered-up. He told me that the night before he sent his letter he had a dream about some conflagration involving his mother in his family home. In the dream she appeared enraged at Alex, but she ended up talking to a wise neighbor/ friend, and the friend calmed her down. The next day Alex was ready to send the letter. Alex sent copies to everyone in the family, those included in the letter and those not included, so that everyone would know what he said.

This is the letter Alex sent:

Dear Family,

I have been collecting my thoughts on this for quite a while, and my trip to North Carolina has given me plenty of time to think. The following letter is not an attack on anyone; please try not to get defensive. I wouldn't write this letter if I didn't love you all so much.

I feel very uncomfortable at our family gatherings, as do my brother and my mother. We hardly ever have family gatherings anymore since father died. I used to love them! Everything was great, and it seemed like everyone got along. It seemed like family, like we were a clan. Now what I see is isolation and people bitching behind other relatives' backs. I think it is because we are all confused about our obligations to my mother.

My father is dead, and my mother suffers from a terrible loss of her physical abilities. You all know that, and I'm sure you all feel awful about it. All I remember was lines of people at the wake passing by me in a blur, all telling me the same thing: "Take care of your mother, you're a man now!" Friends and relatives alike all passed the buck to me—still only a kid.

Do you remember what I was like at sixteen? I was good in school, but other than that I was an IDIOT. I was still a child. I couldn't do anything. I could barely take care of myself! I was fatally shy, and my only responsibility until then was a pa-

thetic nine-customer paper route. *Who said I was a man? All I could do was think about breasts because girls wouldn't even talk to me. WHO GAVE A SHIT ABOUT ME? OR MY BROTHER? I WAS ABSOLUTELY CRUSHED! WHERE THE HELL WERE ALL OF YOU!?? I needed you all, but you weren't there. Nobody ever took a minute to find out how I was doing, or what it was like for me. Instead, all I got was* "So how's your mom doing? You gotta be good and take care of her." *That's all I get now, since the visits to her have tapered off. If you really want to know, you can get the hell over to Arbor Hills Drive and find out for yourself.*

I lost my father and my mother as I knew her. Those pillars of strength were quickly swept from under my feet, and I couldn't do a God-damned thing about it. I was the firstborn son. I was a teenager who needed security, but everything was upside down. I was so scared, I didn't know if we would have any money, or if my mom would hold together, or what my role was. Plus I was hurting so bad nothing even made sense. I was worried about everything. SOMEBODY should have told me not to worry, that my family would be all right.

Did anyone really think I could take care of my crippled family? I unfortunately tried to. I sat in my father's chair at the table. I changed lightbulbs. I let the dog out and locked the doors at night, and I took this responsibility SERIOUSLY. When something went wrong with the car, I went crazy, because I couldn't do anything about it. When my brother was in pain and got into trouble, I was in agony because I wanted to help him, but I couldn't. And when my mother was crying every day, I really wanted to cry, too, but I didn't; I was tough. I would get angry because I was trying desperately to replace my father to make my Mom happy again, but I knew that I was

*falling pathetically short. My Mom tried to help but she was
dependent on me. The only support I got was from a psychologist—a stranger who never even knew me when I was a kid.*

*School, the one thing I was good at, became a joke. My
dreams and my goals were stopped in their tracks. I learned
how to blow off things that were bothering me. Teachers were
asking me why I had so much talent but wasn't trying. I
couldn't tell them because I had no idea myself what was going on. I began to hate myself and actually thought that maybe
I was never really smart to begin with. I could have been vale-
dictorian, but I struggled to stay in the top ten percent. They
kicked me out of National Honor Society because I was getting C's. I felt like I was disappointing everybody.*

*Again, the only person who believed in me was that psy-
chologist. Even my mother wanted me to stay home and told
me I couldn't afford to go away. Of course, no one ever
dreamed of loaning me a little money so I could better myself
through education. EVERYBODY wanted me to go to U.
MASS. NOBODY wanted me to see if I could do better. I got
obsessed with going to Harvard just so I could piss everybody
off. Isn't that kind of a shame?*

*At the college tours and the group information sessions,
every kid there had at least one parent or parent substitute
with them, and most of them had two. But I had to do all the
research on the schools and ask questions myself. While those
other smartest kids looked embarrassed when their dads spoke
up, I asked more questions than anybody.*

*Amherst was the only good place that took me. It is a top-
notch school, and they must have seen that I had potential,
even though I had started to screw up in high school. I was
happy to get in, but I didn't feel like anyone in the family was*

proud of me. I felt like people resented me, after I tried so hard to do something for myself, and I think that is a shame, too.

Everything started catching up with me once I got to Amherst. I shut myself off from friends, I would spend four hours at a time in the library unable to read ten pages, and I was crying all the time. I was in a deep depression and I didn't know why.

I couldn't concentrate at all in college. My mother let me use the car on the condition that I come home at least twice a month to keep an eye on my brother. So I was bribed to take responsibility that shouldn't have been mine. By the way, Greg has had a tough time, too. He is always a little bit sad. He started to act out when he was in high school because of all the shit he had to endure. Instead of empathy, he got Grammy and Grampy shrieking, "How can you be doing this to your poor mother?" Instead of understanding, he was given an enormous amount of guilt. To this day, Greg feels extremely uncomfortable around everybody in his whole family because he thinks you all disapprove of him.

Going to Virginia and getting AWAY from all of this was one of the best things I ever did, but as the dutiful son it was hard to leave. (How could I desert my mother?) I never did that much around the house anyway. I was angry at the way things turned out, at Dad for being dead. I was angry at Mom for being dependent and wanting less than the best for me. And when the rest of the family guilt-tripped me, she only made it worse by amplifying it. But mostly I was mad at myself, for not being Super Boy and fixing everything.

All my friends are now becoming adults, but I feel like I am behind. Even though I have held together enough to get my degree, I have deep regrets that I had a miserable college expe-

rience and that I couldn't put in what was even close to my best efforts. Right now the only way to put together a life for myself is to go away and see who the hell I really am and what I want and what's best for me. Because if I don't do that I will inevitably grow up bitter and either be driven away for good or hating my whole family so much that I do nothing for Mom or myself. I am writing this to give you a chance to keep me. Guilt will not work on me anymore.

I NEED A LIFE!

The next attempt to guilt-trip me into staying home in order for some people to go to California without feeling guilty or for others to generally stay away will not be taken kindly! The primary responsibility for helping my mother rests with her parents and her siblings, and then *with her sons. My mother is doing fine, Grammy and Grampy—all you do is tell me how WEAK my mother is, and how scared she is. She's not weak! Why do you do this? How do you think it makes me feel, you putting down my mother? And I can't believe my mother buys into it.*

I would like to see my family be closer, and I would like to see my mother get some more help if she really needs it. I can't do it right now, okay? I've tried hard enough so far. I want to see less feeling sorry for her and more contact with her. I want to see more love and support. It is not my brother's or my job to do the lion's share of it. *She's got parents and a brother and a sister! What the hell kind of family do we have when no one can count on each other? And when we get mad, we never say anything to that person—everybody just withdraws and stays away and bitches behind their back because they have no guts to come out and just say it. Me included, until now. That just hurts everybody.*

I realize my mother has a serious problem asking for help.

She has stupid pride that makes her feel bad about herself if she asks for help. When you are snotty or act like you're really sacrificing, this condescension will throw her into a rage. She is very sensitive about that. When Grammy comes over and gets all hyper and tells her what to do it throws her into a rage. Do not tell her what to do. Don't treat her like a kid. Be more like a friend. Aunt Molly, when you were nice enough to offer to find someone to rent the house on the lake, Mom thought you were doing her a favor. You then turned around and charged Mom $600. If you ever wonder why Mom doesn't talk to you anymore, there's your answer. This lady watches every penny and makes a new budget every week. You spend money to feel good. I don't know if she'll ever speak to you again.

Read this, but more importantly talk about it to each other. If there's one thing we all do, it is avoid conflict. I do it, too, but it is wrong. I wrote this because I care about my relationships with y'all and your relations with each other. If I didn't care, or didn't have faith in you, I would have left a long time ago and never come back.

The point of this letter is to finally tell you what I am angry about and some things I think the family can do and needs to do to change. Please don't get defensive or try to punish me for being honest and facing what has gone wrong in our family. Please think about what I am saying and feeling and then I would very much like you each to respond—but please do it in a letter (don't call), that way it'll be easier for you and me not to be defensive and to be thoughtful instead.

Love,

Alex

Alex's letter created a firestorm. Nobody wrote; they all called, except his grandparents, who, according to his mother, cried for

days after receiving his letter. His mother called me, understand-
ably angry and upset that I had encouraged Alex to confront the
family. I felt sympathetic to her because I was, indeed, coaching
Alex. I told her I thought that, in the long run, everyone in the
family would benefit from Alex's honesty and I hoped she could
support him.

First, the family members fought, accusing each other and
Alex. Then they started talking, and finally there were attempts at
making up. His aunt, for example, sent his mother the $600 she
had charged her. When his mother, aunt, and grandparents got
angry and defensive, his brother stood up for Alex. So did his
grandmother on his father's side, who was not mentioned in the
letter. The entire family system was shaken up for the better.

His letter was an important turning point for Alex; he felt determined to continue to express his feelings, and he felt tremendously relieved. His depression lifted, his confidence and sense
of competence increased. He felt as if he had taken on a positive
leadership role working toward change in his family. I did, too.

Later that month, Alex wrote me a letter about a conflict we
had in which I had acted as a substitute, intrusive mom. I had
bluntly told him (he had not asked my opinion) that borrowing
money to buy a sports car before leaving the country for six
months was impulsive and a bad idea. Alex's letter was great; he
told me what I had said and done that made him angry and why
he felt misunderstood and unjustly accused. His letter led to an
open discussion, an apology from me, and an admission from him
that he thought my main point was good even though I had been
offensive and relentless in expressing it. Ultimately, his letter led
to a better relationship between us.

12

Responsibility and Blame

A common lay criticism of therapy is that everything gets blamed on the parents. This idea that therapy is a tool to avoid responsibility has gained momentum as research has emerged indicating abuse in a much larger than previously thought portion of the population, and as increased media attention has focused on the issue of repressed memories of abuse that appear only later in life. The use of insanity or victimization as a defense in some highly publicized criminal trials has added impetus to a backlash against the victims of abuse. This backlash has spawned "false memory" groups and given rise to sensationalized media scrutiny of accusers who have invented abuse for their own gain or of those who falsely admit to being perpetrators of abuse.[1]

The view that therapy encourages the therapy client to be a victim and always and unfairly targets the parent as the perpetrator is particularly unfortunate for abused clients. In my experience, these clients have generally hidden or denied abuse at great cost to themselves. Often they already question what they know or remember, and they feel guilty and disloyal for remembering. The backlash bandwagon can encourage and reinforce denial and protection of abusive parents. Until the denial is stopped, the secrets uncovered, and a reality check done to sort out at least some of what really happened in the past, the client cannot take appropriate responsibility for her present situation (stop blaming others for what she is doing and experiencing in her life *now*) and get well.

Psychotherapy works only if the client takes responsibility for how she perpetuates the pattern that keeps her in conflict. To change yourself, you need to get beyond blaming others for what is your responsibility. This does not necessarily mean forgiving others. Nor does it mean failing to hold others responsible or failing to tell them when you do blame them. An essential precursor to taking appropriate responsibility is to avoid being grandiose about responsibility—that is, to stop taking responsibility for everything as if you were the center of the universe.[2] Clients who take too much responsibility and clients who refuse to take any responsibility are unlikely to benefit from insight-oriented therapy or, for that matter, to change in healthy ways.

To take responsibility for what *is* your responsibility, you need to sort out what is *not* your responsibility. The classic example is a child who blames herself for her parents' divorce or for the death of an envied sibling. Since at a certain age, a child sees herself as the center of the universe, her logic is that she causes everything that goes on in her world.

A therapy client may have held herself responsible for her father's sexual advances when she was a child because she wanted her daddy to love her and pay attention to her and to think she was prettier or more wonderful than her mother. Unless she can sort out what was and was not her responsibility, she cannot make a change. She needs to put the responsibility for the lack of appropriate boundaries where it belongs—on the adult. The thinking is, you are not responsible for the original abuse, but you are responsible now (when you are no longer dependent for your survival on your parents) for setting it up for others to abuse you, or for you to abuse yourself, or for you to abuse others. And because you are responsible for perpetuating this rigid abusive pattern, you can change it by changing yourself.

There is a problem here. While cloistered in your therapy session or therapy group, or even in your private life, there is no sure way to sort out what is your responsibility and what is the other person's responsibility. A reality check is necessary. Check with the source. If I blame my husband for something that happened between us, I need to voice what I think and feel to him, the source, to get some further approximation of what really happened. He then has a chance to tell the truth as he sees it, to say what he thinks and feels. This may verify my feelings entirely, in part, or not at all. He may apologize, lie to me, get defensive, attack me, or be open and convince me by his response that I misunderstood him or misperceived his intentions. No matter how he responds, it gives me a reality check because I, like most of my clients, can usually tell a defensive response from an open one, can tell a lie from the truth, and can, when given the other person's point of view, consider it and change my view based on new data.

I cannot get a sense of what really occurred by controlling the world inside my head, by imagining that I am confronting you and imagining your response and my response to your response. I can get a reality check only by letting my feelings, thoughts, and perceptions out into the light and air.

PART IV

Breaking Through Barriers

*Everything secret degenerates . . .
nothing is safe that does not show how it can bear
discussion and publicity.*

—LORD ACTON

13

Letters as a Starting Point for Dialogue

In some families, any expression of feeling is taboo, and family members become increasingly estranged from each other. Even when there is no real abuse or neglect, secrets accumulated in these families commonly destroy communication in ways that have consequences far beyond the immediate vicinity of the original secret. Nevertheless, when family members have the capacity to care about each other and are not severely disturbed, letters can produce significant change in the entire family by starting a dialogue.

Ethan longed to break down the barriers preventing him from getting close to his father. He tried to talk to his father about some of his critical feelings, but he had been keenly sensitive to rejection and felt put off and humiliated by his father's response. Ethan decided to write a letter to his father after he was encouraged in therapy group to get his father out of the box of bad parent in which he had entombed him. He realized that his father was merely flawed, with many good qualities and some bad qualities. In his letter, Ethan was able to bring up issues he had not been able to broach in person, such as his angry feelings about his parents keeping his mother's terminal illness a secret. Ethan's letter and his father's delightfully open response became an immediate springboard for a healthy face-to-face relationship:

Dear Dad,

Serious soul-baring letter of estranged son to father, take 4. I make light of it to make it easier, but it's hard after a lot of years of pretending not to care, or pretending that I can bury my anger and my need, to discover I'm still angry and I still need your love and approval.

Somewhere around age sixteen, I resolved not to show you anymore that I wanted to be close, and now in my thirties I discover the price I paid for faking it—I regret that I've kept you at such a distance, that I haven't been able to accept (except perfunctorily) many of your gifts or to reach out spontaneously on my own. I've hated myself for my own churlishness—even as I've lived with the lingering self-doubt that comes from never having told you how often you hurt me as a child, how seldom you were there when I needed you, how lonely it's been in difficult times not to have a parent I could turn to for love, support, and advice, someone who could tell me I was OK no matter what, that I was important to them because I was me. I am angry and I love you—that those two feelings must be mutually exclusive is the grotesque fallacy I came away with from my childhood: If I was angry I was selfish, and if I was selfish I couldn't love you, and if I didn't love you I deserved the treatment I got—the ignoring, the "go to your room," the put-downs.

In the end, it hasn't been fair to either of us for me to keep my hurts under wraps—hoping that someday maybe you (or someone else) will guess them and make things right—all the while I'm spurning you and anyone else who could really love me.

You'll say I'm being overemotional, or self-pitying, or a martyr, but I want you to see my childhood as I saw it, or as I felt it. Because I don't want you or anyone else to have to guess at my emotions anymore.

Growing up in Providence was hard. The big house, the pool, the servants—drew jealous barbs from my schoolmates; we might as well have had a moat around the place. It was hard to resist the temptations to salve the wounds with thoughts that maybe we were special. It was hard to keep a clear head about our status; I needed to talk to you or Mother about it, but there was never time for that. The flow of visitors—the constant functions—the yearly turnover of nannies—left me feeling lost, unmoored. The house that defined my relations with my peers wasn't mine.

A tighter-knit family might have moored me, but your constant traveling and the priority that university events always took led me to conclude I didn't rate very high in your book. I needed you to say, every so often, "I'm blocking out this time for you, what would you like to do?"

Growing up skinny and unathletic was hard, too. I don't think it had to be that way. I have a painful memory of your taking me out to play catch—I was seven—and after I'd missed the first two throws, you said that was it. The game was over. I had failed. We never played another game—except one croquet match Mother persuaded you to join us in several years later. I needed you to stick with me in that game of catch,

Dad, and to say to me we'd keep practicing because you were sure I could do it. (Imagine my surprise when, in my twenties, I discovered I had the family tennis gene.)

Naturally, your academic success made me expect academic wonders from myself. But it perplexed me that you never took an interest in my grades or my schoolwork. Perhaps it was your way of not putting pressure on me. I needed you to sit down and tell me, at some point, that an academic career was your choice but I'd make my own choice and it would be my choice, but meanwhile you expected me to do my best. I remember when—in tenth grade—I finally had enough A's that I dared to ask you what you thought of my report card. "It was OK," you said, with a don't-be-too-pleased-with-yourself tone. Sometimes I wish you could have got angry with me for selling myself short. Suddenly, I was at boarding school and discovering I was bright: confusion, exhilaration, a chance to redeem myself, and burnout. Then I needed someone to say, it's enough just to do well.

I grew up wondering what was the magic key that would unlock the cell of your disapproval. My room, my clothes, my fingernails, my eating habits, something was always falling short. At the dinner table there was no time for my anecdotes, stories of my friends, and there certainly was no tolerance for my anger. If I raised my voice, the roof fell in. I remember once I got up the courage to run away from you. I'd raised my voice to Mother—not even in anger, more in frustration over something she'd misunderstood—and your terrible "Who do you think you're talking to?" came down like thunder. I ran away, and when I returned you were in an icy sulk. Mother came to me and said, "She couldn't live like this, and I had to apologize." For what? I had to "for her sake." I swallowed my self-respect and did so. You took full advantage, raking me over the coals for my "selfishness." I resent your making me afraid of you; I resent that you made me betray my own conscience; I resent that you'd hurt Mother so. But, most of all, I regret you didn't apologize and show me, by example, that to apologize and to take responsibility for one's actions is to be strong, and to run away from one's actions is weakness.

I think that's when I learned that anger didn't pay and began to pull away, afraid to tell you the truth. Your love seemed to have conditions—that was bad enough, but what made it doubly hard was that you were somehow exempt from the same rules: You could roar; I couldn't even fret. I couldn't raise my voice to Mom—but you'd lock her and the rest of us in the deep freeze. When we moved back, again I needed someone to talk to. We've always talked about your crisis at the university—I had one, too. I lost my friends, my adolescent world.

I know that much of what I missed I might have got if Mother had been stronger. Her physical weakness also, I suspect, forced you into the role of heavy, perhaps oftener than you'd have liked. And since you told me about it last year, I realize you were carrying a terrible psychic burden at that time, knowing how seriously ill she was, and being the only one to know. I don't know that I'd have coped differently. I'm not sure I would have coped with it at all. If you wanted to protect us, I can't blame you. But you weren't the only one who carried the load. The difference was, I didn't know that's what it was.

I drew a child's conclusion that I was unloved because I was unlovable, that the great disorder in the family—holes in the fabric—was somehow my fault.

What makes me sad now is that out of all this I became a kind of play actor—obeying the formalities and never giving any sign of my real anger, keeping you at a distance, never allowing myself to really rejoice in the many generous and thought-

*ful things you've done since those years. I want to be honest
with you. But if I don't write about those things now, it's because I need to exorcize this grudge I've held for too long. I'm
afraid you'll cut me off like you used to. I hope you won't. I
need to know you trust my love for you enough to let me say
what's in my heart.*

Ethan

This letter catapulted Ethan and his father into a newly open
relationship. It was followed by in-person conversations and phone
calls as well as more letter exchanges. Although Ethan had often
talked of his tender and longing relationships with men and his
difficulties with women as romantic partners, he had not felt
ready to tackle his sexual identity. About a year and a half after
this first up-front letter to his father, Ethan figured out that he
was homosexual. He had very little difficulty "coming out," in
large part because he had had the courage to face the difficult
feelings he had about his father and to work out that relationship.
Because of this solid relationship, Ethan predicted he could talk
comfortably with his father about his sexual identity and that his
father would accept him. Happily, his prediction was accurate.

················

Richard had worked hard and productively to understand his
conflictual relationship with his mother. He was financially dependent on her even though he was in his mid-fifties. He made
many breakthroughs in therapy without ever really confronting
his mother. During a recent visit he had an interaction with her
about a pivotal time in their family history. This so crystallized his
feelings of anger that he easily put them into writing. He had
never been so direct with his mother. Often when people try out
a new behavior, the new behavior lacks grace and nuance. In the

long run, though, it is better to err on the side of even a strident communication than to muffle and perhaps bury bad feelings:

Mom:

During your weekend here I realized how angry I am with you. . . . You told me that you didn't take Sally and me to France because you couldn't take us away from our father. You spoke as if you wanted me to thank you, to be sorry for you.

. . . You expressed surprise that I had known of your plans. How could you imagine that I did not know something was wrong. . . . You brought Pierre back from France to live in our home, where you fucked him and, in doing so, fucked us all. . . . You stood in the living room and announced that you were pregnant. At least Dad had the balls to say it wasn't his child.

My anger now is not whether you took us to France or fucked Pierre. My anger is that you have been so focused on yourself, filled with self-pity. Even today you are seeking my thanks and sympathy for having sacrificed for us when you fucked us over, Dad included.

You raised the subject when you were here. I am glad that you did. If you want to continue to address it, I suggest that you respond to this letter in writing.

Richard

The return letter from his mother made it clear that she was truly shocked that her son had been aware of her "secret" affair with Pierre. In her letter, she covertly requested that if his sister did not already know these secrets she be kept in the dark. The rest of her letter was dramatically self-blaming, but with so much hyperbole that it did not act as a bridge or a real apology. Richard's response letter follows.

Mom:

   I am sad that I did not confront you years ago.

   Your letter makes my point. You responded with lots of drama and focus on your suffering. You write, "How can I say I am sorry?" Just say it.

   In fact, your letter crystallizes how we have connected and colluded with each other in the past.

   You responded seductively with "you of all people would know . . . Sally, too?" Of course Sally must know. Do you think I am smart and Sally is dumb? I feel like you are trying to split us, to appeal to my past willingness to collude with you in your criticism of Sally, of Dad, of Ted. Your exaggerated flattery of me—direct and indirect—is a long-baited trap.

   You responded rhetorically with "I thought forever I was getting away with something—and I didn't see what I could be doing to my children. . . ." Come on. How could you not know?

   I am appalled that you want to thank me "for suffering [you] so long." I do not want your thanks.

   You should be appalled that I suffered you so long and colluded with you so much, that I wanted your thanks. I am appalled that I did so.

   I am also relieved that I have begun to confront my anger and we have begun to talk. I would like to continue doing so in writing at this time.

Richard

P.S. I am sending copies of our letters to Sally and Ted

   In response to this letter, his mother left a message on his answering machine warning him that he would regret it if he sent copies of his letters to his sister and foster brother. The giving up of old secrets is hard, and his mother was threatened when he insisted that their exchange include his siblings. For Richard, it was the only way to stop colluding with his mother and the only way to bridge the distance he had always felt between his sister and himself over competition for his mother's favor.

Since these two brief letters Richard has been able to keep talking frankly to his mother. Although Richard had realized before that having his mother bail him out of financial difficulties was his passive way of being angry at her, this realization had not helped him let go of his hostile, dependent connection to her. His letters did the trick. Getting his anger out to his mother, particularly around old secrets, had a direct effect on his financial and emotional well-being. He started making a great deal of money. He won an award in his company for how much business he pulled in. If he does get into financial trouble again, it seems clear that he will not go to his mother to bail him out. When he wrote his mother citing the specifics of what he was angry about, he severed his dependent connection to her, creating room for a new and better relationship to develop.

Richard's mother was recently hospitalized with a broken hip, and he went to spend the weekend with her to help in her care. They talked openly and without rancor. He reported that his mother struck him for the first time as interesting and intelligent.

....

Dottie (whose draft response is found in Chapter 5) would not have confronted her mother if her problems with her mother had not been interfering with her relationship with her husband. She was habitually angry at both of them for not taking her seriously. The relationship of her anger to secrets would become apparent only later.

Dear Mom,

I am writing this letter to free myself so that I can be a better wife and mother and have a better relationship with you. I am also writing this for Sandra so that I don't pass along the same messages to her.

I have a pact with you: I can't be any happier with my life than you are with yours. I can't feel really good about Edward because that would violate our pact. You wanted me to mirror your feelings, and if I didn't I paid for it. I've been trying all my life to get something I've never gotten from you. I never felt as if I got the nurturing and loving I needed without conditions attached. If I didn't match your feelings the nurturing was withheld, and I never knew why because I didn't know the rules.

. . . Because you wanted a special bond with me, you never taught me how to be friends with anyone else, especially boys. I got the message that I shouldn't get too close to anyone because they would leave me or let me down, but you wouldn't let me down. I had to be nice to everyone though. It didn't matter how I felt about them or how it affected me. I wasn't supposed to like them too much or get too close, but I was supposed to be "friendly," which made me feel phony and uncomfortable. You never taught me that I could say no to anyone. That wouldn't be nice.

The only way I knew how to be close to men or boys was with physical closeness. But I wasn't supposed to have sex, but how could I not have sex without saying no. . . . You made me feel that pleasure through touching or sexual feelings was wrong, and the message became "don't feel pleasure (any pleasure) or allow others to pleasure me (in any way)."

You gave me bad lessons as to how to get what I wanted. I

learned not to ask outright for anything—be coy, shy, naive, and secretive. Expect to get what you want but don't ask for it. I learned not to be honest. The things and feelings I needed to talk about most and get support for I didn't talk about and I still don't.

I got the message that men are not worth much. They have to be protected and taken care of. I remember you saying often, "don't tell your father," as if he wouldn't be able to handle whatever it was we weren't to tell him. How do you think it made me feel to hear those messages about men and Dad specifically? . . . It affects how I feel and think about Edward. I feel as if I can't be myself, and I also feel and expect that he will only disappoint me.

I feel alone and lonely most of the time, and I think it's because I'm still trying to keep the attachment with you. That makes me angry with you, so I don't feel close to you and you can never do anything right for me because I'm angry. What a vicious cycle!

. . . I remember you telling me about my old boyfriend Roger getting killed right after college graduation. You just dropped the news and went on to something else. . . . When I told you I needed some time to deal with the news, you acted as if you were surprised I had any feelings about it at all. That's a big part of the problem for me. . . . Good or bad, I couldn't have my own feelings.

. . . I grew up wanting to have a man. More than friends, more than anything else. How did I get the message that I needed one so badly? Why was it so important to me?

These are some of the things that still affect me today. Take some time and write me back. I will call you after I get your response. It's been very hard for me to write this to you, but

I want a better relationship with you and I think it will help.

Love,

Dottie

When Dottie received a return letter, she was both relieved and disappointed by the response. She was relieved that her mother was not defensive and disappointed that her mother still did not seem interested in really knowing her. She perceived her mother as being open to realizing that she had not been a good mother and open to the ways she had failed but, like Richard's mother, more focused on herself and feeling sorry for herself than on changing her behavior toward Dottie:

Dear Mom,

Thank you again for your letter. I have to say I think it proves you are very wise in many ways and very courageous. Most people would have responded angrily and defensively, but you really took me seriously and looked at yourself very openly.

. . . As for what you can do differently, the main thing is being interested in me. Knowing me as a person with my own feelings and accepting me for who I am. An example of what I mean is what you didn't put in your letter. Your letter . . . told me a lot about your feelings and thoughts, but you didn't ask any questions about my feelings. I would like for you to ask me about parts of my letter that you might not have understood, or more about how I felt at the time, or how those things affect me now. I know you sometimes see that as prying, but I can always tell you if I don't want to get into something.

I know you feel guilty and I think that's good if it motivates a change in your behavior with me. It isn't good if it keeps you focused on you rather than on me. I think I misled you by saying (when we talked) that we want the same thing from each other. I was trying to make you feel better about not having had interest in me as a little girl. I did what I often do, which is to smooth things over and make it easier for you. I want you to take care of me as a mother now, not as a sibling or as a friend. I want . . . to be your daughter.

Love,
Dottie

Dottie's letter opened a door, but the door slowly started to close again. Her mother remained entrenched in old self-focused behavior, and Dottie fell back into disappointed passivity. Dottie felt less tense with her mother because she had expressed herself honestly, but for reasons I was unaware of at the time, she was unwilling to sustain the effort required to keep the relationship growing.

It was over a year later when Dottie realized that the sexual molestation she had suffered (and never repressed) as an eight-year-old from the janitor at school and then the next year from her uncle on her father's side was related to her continued depression. She came to understand that she was angry at her mother, who learned about the abuse by the uncle shortly after it happened. When Dottie had tried to talk to her mother about it, her mother pretended it hadn't happened and wouldn't talk to Dottie. After this Dottie kept it secret, too. The uncle was later jailed for molesting children. Dottie was particularly enraged when she was at her uncle's funeral and her mother asked did she remember him.

It took Dottie continued work on herself to understand that she kept failing to ask for what she wanted from her mother, her husband, or anyone because she felt she did not deserve to get pleasure or attention. She had internalized bad feelings about herself, blaming herself for the sexual abuse she had experienced because she wanted attention from the janitor and from her uncle.

Dottie recently invited her parents to a family session (she asked her husband to come to support her) in which she confronted her mother and father about the sexual abuse and her mother's lack of response to it. She also confronted her father about his sexualized relationship with her. At this session her mother said that she "forgot" that she ever knew the uncle abused Dottie. When Dottie told her parents about the janitor, her mother revealed that she had been sexually molested by the ice man when she was nine and never told anyone until she told her husband a year earlier.

The session was a great relief to Dottie. She was very direct with her parents; she expressed her anger and her criticisms. She was specific about how her father was inappropriately close to her and how her mother both set this up and was angry and jealous at the same time. When her parents tried to avoid or deny, Dottie called this out, with some help from me and her husband, and asked that her parents try again to take her seriously. They did. She told all her secrets. She left feeling less angry and more understanding both of herself and them.

....

Needing to keep a secret or fearing that someone will tell on you can ruin relationships unnecessarily. Often, as in Richard's or Dottie's family, the secret keeping does as much or more harm than the "sin" that occasioned the secret. When Brenda became clear about the role secrets played in her life, her inability to give credit to others where credit was due, and the role competition with female peers (often over father figures) played, she wrote a

letter to Mr. Edmonds. Mr. Edmonds had acted as a surrogate father to her when her own father died. Brenda had been keeping
her secret because she was afraid Mr. Edmonds was angry at her.
Her fear had prevented her from telling him how grateful she was
to him. This was her first communication with Mr. Edmonds in
over two decades, and it underscores how confronting the truth
by letter can take the form of "thank you's" as easily as it can take
the form of criticisms.

Dear Mr. Edmonds,
    This letter—part thank you, part confession, part apology—
is long overdue.
    My own father died when I was seven. He smoked and
drank too much. In my last memories of him, he was over-
worked and pasty-faced. I watched you ice skate outside the
big window of your house, and I knew you weren't going to die
on me. You were the sturdiest, most energetic adult I had ever
seen. It's impossible for me to imagine that you can't walk ten
times faster and longer than I can, even now. . . .
    You were ambitious for me. When I was nine, I fell off a
horse at a horse show. . . . You wanted me to get right back up
on a horse, to get over it. I was ashamed at having fallen, but
because you were encouraging me, I got back up. I even rode
bareback at your house. You made me feel I could do it. You
wanted me to open myself up to new worlds. To this day I as-
sociate certain foods with you because you got me to try them
for the first time. They are my favorite foods: sourdough bread,
crab meat, lobster, and artichokes. When I was at my most self-
involved, sulking phase of adolescence, you encouraged me to
pick my head up and look around me. I was so much more
open with you than with my own family. I wanted to tell you
everything. It was a privilege to be with a grown-up who

wanted to discuss important ideas and who had clear opinions about the world. Don't make the same mistakes I made, you told me: Sleep with your boyfriend before you get married. Learn to drive a car, so you can get home if your date has too much to drink. Take care of yourself.

Your political views were different from my parents': You suggested to me that action was as important a quality for a leader as analysis. Adlai Stevenson is too intellectual, you said; he couldn't make up his mind about anything. Eisenhower was the better politician. It wasn't the content of what you said, it was the fact of your engaging with me as an equal, arguing with me, taking my responses seriously. Now that I am a teacher I see clearly how lucky I was to have had you as a teacher.

Now for the hard part.

I talked to Nadine for the last time when I was a sophomore in college. There was a lot of unspoken tension between us. In the course of our conversation, I used the expression "capitalist pig" . . . she thought I was talking about you. She was furious. It was unlike her to be furious; she was usually polite and extremely restrained. I had hit a nerve. "How dare you talk about capitalist pigs after all my father has done for you!" She defended you to the hilt. I insisted I wasn't implicating you. She insisted I was—you were capitalist; I had referred to capitalists as pigs. We had a political argument, which was silly. We needed to be having a personal argument. She was closer to saying what was on her mind than I was. She had shared you with me. I had cared more about you—pleasing you, talking to you, being with you—than I had cared about her. More than that, I had competed with her: I wanted to be a better daughter to you, more open, more interested in what you were interested in than she was. And now, the final betrayal: Here I was glibly talking about "capitalist pigs" as though you didn't matter.

It was the last conversation she and I ever had.

I worked at your company the summer after my junior year in college. I sent a note up to your office on the top floor, via your secretary. When you didn't answer the note, I imagined that Nadine had told you I called you a capitalist pig. I was paranoid. I wondered if you got the note. Then I stewed about it.

If you had gotten the note, it would have seemed cold and distant. You had asked me to call you "uncle." What was I doing sending you a note, like an employee? If I had had the courage of my convictions, I would have bounded up the elevator and insisted on seeing you. If you hadn't been there, I should have called you. Even if you were angry with me, it would have been better for me to know it than to lose touch with you. I never found out what you thought about my disappearing from your life. Did Nadine tell you she didn't want you to have anything to do with me? Did you hate me? Did you mistrust me? I would like to know.

One of the last memories I have of being with your family is playing a trust game in your living room. We joined hands. One person had to fall and trust the others to hold them up. I knew your family was falling apart. You were struggling and looking for ways to stay together. You were trying: clinics, therapies. I admired your activism. I was glad to be there with you.

For a fatherless kid, I felt like the luckiest kid because of you. The privilege of being let in on your world, your conversation, the knowledge you shared, your high expectations for me, gave me a confidence in myself that I've carried with me in my work ever since. You've been a resource for me all this time. I have a longstanding problem with suspicion and keep-

ing things secret! I've let go of a lot of good things in my life because of not having it out with people when I needed to. Losing touch with you is one of my biggest regrets—and I blame myself for not fighting openly with Nadine and not staying in touch with you when that was what I really wanted.

This letter of thanks has been two decades too long in coming. I hope it's not too late to hear from you.

Love,
Brenda

P.S. I'm sending you my articles. You don't have to read them! I want you to have them because you were so important in helping me grow up and encouraging me to be active in the world. In that way you've influenced these articles.

Brenda received a warm letter from Mr. Edmonds by return mail and later an invitation to visit Mr. Edmonds and his daughter. His daughter had never told her father of their conversation, and in his letter he indicated that he was not now and would not then have been offended by Brenda's remarks to his daughter. The twenty-year barrier was down.

....

Rebecca's mother and father were Holocaust survivors. Rebecca's father became severely depressed and committed suicide when Rebecca was in her teens. Rebecca and her mother had a loving relationship, but Rebecca felt burdened because her mother constantly worried about her daughter's welfare and repeatedly told her that she (the mother) couldn't be happy unless Rebecca was happy. She could not tell her mother how oppressive this was to her.

Rebecca decided to write a letter home. Her group told her

that her first draft sounded like she was a mother talking down to her child. She realized that she had always felt that she needed to take care of her mother, since her mother seemed not to be taking care of herself. Her revised letter was forthright without being whiny or abrasive. Her mother was very distressed by the letter but took it seriously and responded openly. This led to good talks, and they became much closer. In spite of this, Rebecca's second letter home was the most difficult letter Rebecca had ever written. She wrote it with no commitment to send it. Even when she decided she wanted to send the letter, she delayed sending it for several months because she knew her mother would be extremely upset about the revelations in the letter and she wanted to protect her mother:

Warning: Enclosed Material May Be Difficult to Read
Dear Meem,

Because you have responded so well to me when I've had the courage to be honest with you (including even your response to the letter I gave you last December, which you hated), and because I feel closer to you when I can be honest with you, I want to tell you some important developments in my life, so that you will fully know me. The main thing to tell you is that I am attracted to women and am now in a relationship with one.

The background is that in my past relationships with men, I never felt that I could be completely myself. I was always repressing parts of myself that might threaten them, or that they might not understand. I was trying to fit my being into a mold that was too small for it. . . . I was trying to clip my wings and settle for something that wasn't the real thing. Then, a few years ago, I became attracted to a woman and knew that I'd found a profound part of myself I needed to explore. I knew this would be hard, for it meant overcoming my fears, breaking out of my safe circle of friends, taking new emotional risks. I did it anyway. In the process, I began relationships with two women who were not right for me. Then I met Sylvia, with whom I began a relationship in May. As we've gotten to know each other, our appreciation for one another has grown and deepened; we also have a lot of fun together. As you know, she's spending the fall semester in Japan.

In January we can start to see each other again and find out whether there is something lasting here; it's far too early to tell now. What I can tell you is that those unexpressed parts of myself have found a place to go where they can be seen, appreciated, and honored. I have never been so happy. Yet I'm not blinded by love; I'm keeping my feet on the ground and getting a realistic picture of Sylvia over time.

Ever since our relationship began, I've been wanting to tell you, both because it's such a great happiness for me and because I don't want to keep things from you. I've felt caught between the possibility of upsetting you and the intolerable situation of hiding something so important from you. I've also been afraid of your reaction. And I still am. But I've chosen to tell you because I want us to keep having the same authentic relationship we always have had.

You've often remarked in recent years—including this past summer—that I was doing better than ever physically and mentally. You've even said in your letter of last week that I'd become wise. This ability to really love is part of that larger process of flowering. I'm more open in every way, to new ideas, to people, to fun. I see it in my teaching, my writing, even in administration. This feeling of openness and of being centered also comes from tenure and professional recognition. It all works together as part of a general process of being healthier and becoming who I really am. It will sound strange, but I think of the Yom Kippur portion "Behold, I have set before you this day good and evil, life and death; choose life. . . ." For me, choosing this love is choosing life.

To give you an idea of what Sylvia's like, she has some of Hanna's ability to think and feel at the same time, and some of Dana's wit and soulfulness. She's a sociologist who spent last year on a fellowship and will be teaching here in January. I could of course go on and on about her, but this is not the time. When you have questions about her, just ask. And of course, if this lasts, I'd like you to get to know her.

It's easy for me to imagine that you will be wondering whether you did something wrong as a mother. In fact, you made me into a considerate, honest person with an ability to love and to deal with difficult challenges. And when I look back at my life, I know that this is who I was from birth. It has nothing to do with how you raised me, or with Daddy's death. It's just who I am. And I guess the most important thing I want you to know is that I'm the same person I have always been; this part of me that has been masked has always been part of the whole me, even when I couldn't acknowledge it.

I also want you to know that I've been fortunate to come to this realization in a community and a university which are extremely supportive. This area has one of the largest gay communities in the country and has social groups for professional women who hold potluck lunches once a month at someone's house. As for my university, there are many tenured, influential gay and lesbian faculty, and the university has instituted a policy that provides benefits to same-sex partners. However, I have not made this public, since I consider it part of my private life and at the moment have no interest in working in gay studies, which are all the rage on the campus.

I'm looking forward to talking to you about this whenever it feels right to you, on the phone, via mail, and eventually in person at Christmas. You can take your time to respond if you like; all I want to know right away is that you have received this letter. I chose to write rather than telling you in person so that you could reread this whenever you wanted to, and so that you would have a chance to react in your own time.

Love,
Rebecca

Initially Rebecca's mother was devastated, angry, and shocked. In response to Rebecca's letter, she made very prejudiced and naive statements about homosexuality. Rebecca expected this. With a little help from her friends, Rebecca stayed remarkably undefensive. Over a period of many months they argued and talked and finally worked it out. When her mother came to visit, she met Sylvia. During her mother's stay, Rebecca gave a party for her friends—gay and straight. After the party, Rebecca's mother admitted she had had a good time and that she could not tell the gay from the straight women. When Rebecca and Sylvia broke up the following year, Rebecca's mother was genuinely upset for her. Rebecca was touched and surprised when her mother said she thought that Sylvia had been good for her in many ways.

14

Dialoguing with Letters

Dave is the oldest son of a renowned neurologist. He has two brothers and one sister. Although his father was abusive to all his children, Dave was singled out because his father had pinned most of his hopes on him. The early drafts of Dave's first letter were garbled and indirect. He wrote in long Germanic sentences. He used esoteric and psychologically sophisticated language, and between the lines he was condescending. If he had sent those first drafts he would have ensured a defensive and hostile response. He could thus have proved himself right in his view of his father as total villain and his mother as seductive saint.

After many revisions, Dave wrote a good first letter confronting his father with the abuse he and his brothers and sister had sustained. Once he mustered the courage to send it, he no longer felt terrified of his father. When his father responded to that letter, Dave wrote the other letters in the series with ease. There was only one exception: When Dave got a particularly adoring note from his mother, he told his group he felt hopeful and relieved that she was finally beginning to deal with the issues he raised in his letters. He had said as much in his draft response to her letter. His group had him take a second look at both his mother's note and his response to it. It became clear to Dave that he had been seduced by her flattery again. It was a breakthrough for him; he realized that flattery was his Achilles' heel with women, even women he did not much like.

Dave was then able to write his mother a straightforward letter. Had he not taken the time to get feedback from his friends, he would have stopped himself from getting clear, and he could easily have fallen back into the old, bad pattern with his mother. This initial slip may account for the relentless, hard-edged quality of his letters to his mother.

Dave's letters home resulted in a real dialogue with his father. The letters to and from his mother, on the other hand, belong in the "butting heads" category. The series of letters Dave wrote to his father provides a contrast to Cindy's and Susanna's letters. Although Dave's father was defensive, he was able to drop his defensiveness at times. I have included the entire sequence of Dave's letters to illustrate the dialogue that can be initiated by the first letter and the progression in Dave's and his father's relationship as the dialogue unfolds. This particular exchange is still in progress.

1. Dear Dad and Mom,

Dad—it's perplexing you have no idea what's "troubling" me. Your letter appears to have been written like it was from a father who genuinely cared for and loved me. The reality of your actions is wholly different. . . . Mom—you failed to provide me any protection against Dad's abusiveness and instead seduced me with "secrets" (like giving me money behind Dad's back to make me "feel" better and confiding in me how weak and terrible Dad was/is). . . . Dad, since you asked, here are the "problems" as I see them.

You constantly threatened physical abuse and consistently humiliated me (and the other kids). The fact that you never carried out most of these threats made them even worse because I was left in a constant state of terror and felt as if I had no control over my own safety. When Theo and I got caught lighting matches down by the creek, you threatened to burn our fingertips with your cigar to teach us a lesson. Or telling us that we would have to run around the house naked in winter if we didn't stop misbehaving as young children. Or making us lie down on your bed with our pants down so you could whip us with your belt. Or when you put your pistol in your mouth and threatened to "blow your head off" because you didn't "know what to do with me." Or when you threatened to "shove every inch of winch cable over fifteen feet up Gerald's ass" when he lied to you about how much he broke off. Despite your supposed "love and respect," we were treated like scum. I can't think of a single instance with you that wasn't contaminated with my feeling terrified of you becoming enraged and abusive. . . .

What is also beyond my comprehension is how you could do things so gravely inappropriate as holding Theo and me up over your head while we were in the shower with you to wash our ass holes out with the shower like it was some kind of fun game. Also, the "medical" exams where you inspected my genitals for no medical reason. Like when I was sick in bed at Gram's and Gramp's or when I needed a physical for graduate school. Where were you during all this, Mom?

The ways you (Mom) didn't protect me amounted to seducing me with secrets to appease and thwart my anger at Dad (and you). You used situations where he was most abusive to collude with me by privately siding with me, but not standing up to him. That you continually deal with things indirectly shows me you really know what's going on. . . . I have had to secretly negotiate with you to get time to develop relationships and pursue goals independent of you and Dad. Since it is "normal" for everything to revolve around Dad's schedule and demands, the best way for me to get time to myself was by making secret deals with you. . . .

I remember you pleading with me to spend time with Dad working outside when I was plainly not interested in doing chores on Christmas Eve. In coercing me to participate in Dad's workaholic routine, you teasingly mentioned that "Dad thinks this is his last year," without explanation. It was much more extreme when you, Mom, later said how inappropriate it was for you to give Dad a handgun for Christmas when he was feeling suicidal. I deeply regret I didn't ask you what you were talking about on either occasion . . . on one hand, you were telling me to take this seriously, but on the other, you were joking around. I felt in a terrible bind, like you were forcing me to deal with it instead of you. Whatever your intentions, it's a hostile way to make Dad powerless and weak.

My entire relationship with both of you has been fraught with fear, humiliation and deceit. . . . My life is much happier without you in it. Any meaningful relationship with either of you would require tremendous change on both your parts.

Since my experience of you (Dad) is that you don't listen to what I have to say if it is not in complete agreement with how you see things, I am not hopeful of any response. However you take this, I'm glad you asked because it is important for my own clarity to name these horrors. If you choose to discuss any of this with Theo, Gerald, or Sally, I will send them a copy of this letter so that they know exactly what I am saying to you. I will also send them a copy if they express an interest in knowing what I have said to you. I prefer any response from you (both of you) to be by letter.

Dave

Writing this first letter home had a profound influence on Dave. In group therapy and in the couples work he did with his girlfriend before he started group, he realized that he was angry most of the time. He found it almost impossible to speak his mind when he disagreed with or felt critical of someone close to him. He understood in an intellectual way that this kept him from being intimate and made him feel burdened by the demands of his friends, girlfriend, parents, therapist, or teacher. He had vaguely blamed his parents for his unhappiness, but he had not made the connection between his fear of speaking up to his parents and the inhibition that kept him masked and therefore angry. Once he wrote this first letter, he understood that as long as he continued to mask his feelings and opinions he would remain an angry young man who leaked out his anger in self-destructive ways. In group, for example, he would entrap people into giving him advice or help he didn't really need or want and then would get angry that we discounted him by thinking he needed so much help.

Even before he got a response to his letter, Dave's work in therapy changed; he began to feel that the locus of control for his life was in him, not in others. He became more trustworthy in group. When he did fall back into tricky behavior and the group challenged him, he was relieved rather than angry:

2. *Dear Mom,*
   I got your letter, and I'm extremely disappointed. . . . You're trying to cut me off at the pass. Since you "want to start from

*today," it's clear to me that you're plainly not interested in what
I have to say. . . . What's even worse is that you tried to shut me
up with all that Christian sugary shit. To think I ever bought
it sickens me.*

Dave

3. Dear Dad and Mom,

*Dad . . . I appreciated your willingness to take responsibil-
ity for your psychologically abusive ways. Mom—I am disappointed that you have not responded. The rest of this letter is
primarily addressed to you, Dad, since you did respond. Mom,
my hope is that you will read it also.*

*After reading your letter, I am left with a feeling very simi-
lar to what I experienced during the calm after the storm during times when you would yell unmercifully at me. Many
times after such episodes you would say that you were overre-
acting because you were interested in helping me "realize my
full potential". . . . It seemed to me that if this were the case
you would not scream the devastating put-downs at me that
you did, nor would you pose the terrifying threats that you did.
My safety felt in constant jeopardy, even after your stormy rage
subsided. Despite my repeated and misguided attempts to do
the "right" thing (thanks to you, Mom), I felt alone and helpless in trying to protect myself. The feeling that you could ex-
plode again at any future moment in a totally unpredictable
way was always in the back of my mind. And it still is when I
read your recent letters.*

*I am very dismayed at your attempt to exonerate Mom. Her
unwillingness to deal with your abusive ways made the situation much worse. Her unwillingness to respond is a major
roadblock in any future relationship . . . and now you're pro-*

tecting her by taking her out of the picture. I experienced her attempts to cover up the abusive ways you treated me as devastatingly confusing. It made it extremely difficult for me to make any sense out of the fear I felt, or understand the problems in our family. . . . I see her efforts to "maintain an equilibrium" as prolonging the problems.

It was inappropriate for you to have performed the physical examinations, whatever the reason. Do your colleagues perform such examinations on their children? . . .

I disagree with your point that our communication process is faulty. At least now the horrors are out in the open. . . . I do not fully trust your response, given my past experience of your excessive apologies after situations when you were abusive. I strongly believe that if I were to agree to start anew at this point and get on with our relationship, the problems would resurface in a very short time. . . . I don't see that a quick resolution is possible given the extent and magnitude of the problems in our relationship, but as I said at the outset, I found your response heartening. . . . I still prefer any response (from either of you) to be by letter.

Dave

Dave was surprised, given how initially terrified he was of challenging his father, that his dad was at all open about himself (with the exception of the implied sexualized behavior). He was equally surprised by his mother's closed responses. He had always believed her to be the more loving parent.

4. Dear Mom and Dad,

Mom, I received your letter and my response is primarily addressed to you, although it is again my hope that you will both read it. (Dad, I've enclosed a copy of Mom's letter in case you didn't see it.) Mom—I was surprised that you are under the impression that I am "experiencing terrible pain." Quite the contrary . . . I experience having things out in the open as a relief. Instead of feeling pain because you imagine I'm suffering, I would rather you feel pain for your complicity in the problems.

I agree with you that the separation when you were pregnant with Theo is not significant. However, I was disappointed that you do not address any of the "real issues". . . . You only offer prayer for "healing and restoration". . . . Your pledge that "change is coming" seems empty. How am I to know that change is "happening" when I see no evidence of it? You cover up the issues I raised by emphasizing faith and religion. It is reminiscent of the very real way you separated yourself from me while I was growing up by becoming intensely involved with Christianity, instead of dealing with the problems in our family.

. . . You try to console me by saying that I'm more intelligent and more astute than Theo and Gerald, pitting me against them and putting them down (they "need" a swat) in the interest of trying to make me feel special and shut me up once again. It is disappointing that you are still trying to "buy" me off with excessive and seductive flattery, especially after I have accused you of using flattery to shut me up and collude with you to ignore major problems instead of deal with them. I find it appalling that I could have been so easily directed in the ways you admit to. You describe this as being an "especially sensitive person". . . .

Your ending . . . feels like a last-ditch effort for me to once again collude with you. . . .

Dave

Note that Dave has become aware that not only was his mother's relationship with him based on flattery but that it depended on raising Dave's self-esteem by putting his dad down or, in a pinch, his brothers.

5. *Dear Dad and "invisible" Mom,*

   It seems ridiculous to me to try to spend Christmas together "as a family" when Mom has not dealt with any of what I've said. You've made a start in your responding (and it's much better than any I can remember), but . . . you still refuse to deal with Mom's lack of response.

   Your card makes it sound like there have been no letters at all. You have been responding, and me back, and now you've wiped that out. My impression is that our letters to each other have been productive because they've been clear, up-front, and open. However, you say things like "further I see no resolution with letter writing" or ". . . there needs to be a first step." . . . I feel bad because you're acting as if nothing good has happened.

                                                                 Dave

At this point Dave needed help from his group to keep differentiating his mother's vapid responses from his father's substantive responses, because his father tried to cover up his wife's inadequacies by speaking for both of them. We needed to remind Dave that his letters home created difficulties for his father beyond having to face how he had been a bad parent in the past. His father wanted to repair his relationship with his son without causing a rift in his relationship with his wife. This was particularly problematic because his wife was quickly losing her status as the warm and loving parent who buffered David from his evil father. Dave understood from his parents' response letters that the truth was far more complex than he had imagined when he started writing letters home.

6. *Dad,*

You seem to be taking charge to protect Mom, yet from my perspective it feels like you're putting her down by treating her as a nonentity who is incapable of responding. . . . If she is doing the best that she can, I need to know that for myself.

Mom,

You and Dad are acting as if I only have issues with him, like I haven't had anything to say to you. . . . It saddens me to face the possibility that the only relationship I have with you is based on the embers of my relationship with Dad. I need to know. . . .

Dave

7. *Dear Mom,*

. . . You have not seemed "invisible" because you haven't written but because your offerings have been empty. Unfortunately, the only way that you seemed at all visible is when you act wounded ("rebuffed and refuted"). I feel totally boxed in— my choices appear to be to further "wound" you by giving you my real reaction to what you have written, to go along with your responses as if it is a meaningful offering, or to just give up the possibility of having any sort of meaningful relationship with you. . . . The only changes have been on the surface (like not using the "cute" stationery and giving a copy to Dad).

Your "efforts to appease and moderate" have felt anything but loving. I'm surprised that you would think that it would help to know that Gramp made the same secret deals with you—I would have thought that you'd have learned how bad that must have been for your relationship with Gram, and with him. Loving me "too much" and hoping that love will "prevail in healing" seems empty . . . in the same way I've been pointing out. You haven't heard me say how bad this has been for me in the past. . . . I can't have a sincere and honest relationship with you based on that kind of love.

. . . Because my only "fond" memories of times with you do not involve Dad at all . . . it leaves me with the impression that the good times with you were based on things being bad with Dad, or him plainly not being there, and that is how my relationship with you feels empty. What are the "wonderful and fun" times you remember? Can you remember any when Dad was in the picture? . . .

Dave

8. *Dear Dad,*

. . . Your letters have meant a lot. . . . I chalk this up to me hanging in there and saying what I have been mad about in a way unlike my destructive behavior in the past and to you persisting in progressing to work out our relationship, and I am truly grateful for your efforts.

I too would like to start to talk face to face, and I agree with you that face-to-face discussion with professional counseling is the best first step. My only worry is that it seems as if you and Mom come as a package deal. I am not optimistic that she is open to this in the way you are. . . . I would like to work things out with both of you, but I . . . may only be able to work things out with you. I hope you can accept this possibility, at least as a start. Since it might take a while to set up counseling, I hope that in the meantime she would try to respond to . . . my letters to her so that she could at least be in the ballpark when we meet.

It would be better for me if we could make some arrange-

ments in this area. I will check into some possibilities down here, and I would like to hear your thoughts on this.

Thanks for the photos and the article on our basketball team. Did you see the . . . game?

Love,

Dave

9. *Dear Mom,*

. . . I'm not sure how to take your note . . . when you keep saying "we" and "we'll" try—I have no idea what you are planning to try. . . . If you really want to try . . . reread my letters and address the points I have raised. No platitudes. The way to try is to say something specific. The impression I get is that you have only given my letters a cursory read and haven't really listened to what I have said.

Love,

Dave

10. *Dear Dad,*

With each of your letters I feel more hopeful that we can work out our relationship. I appreciate your openness toward counseling and your willingness to come down here. I agree with you that when you do come, it would be nice to spend time together (in addition to counseling), but I'd rather not try to make up for the lost years of you not being interested in (or putting down) "my professional activities." I'd rather not have this pressure imposed on either of us. . . .

. . . You sound so determined for me to be satisfied with Mom's lack of response when you say we "must" work things out. . . . If feels like a real attack on my perceptions for you to say I should understand just because "she loves me," and imply

that the fact she hasn't offered a meaningful response shouldn't matter. . . .

. . . Right now, a counseling session for all three of us would be unproductive, not to mention how awkward things would feel for the remaining visit if she were excluded from a counseling session where you and I worked on our relationship and got closer. I hope that you don't have to wait for Mom to work out our differences—I don't have to resolve things with her to resolve things with you. . . .

Love,

Dave

11. *Dear Dad & Mom,*

YOU'RE BOTH NOT LISTENING!

. . . Why are you speaking for Mom again? . . . Mom, I am puzzled that you (and you too, Dad) imply that I suggested your marriage is somehow in jeopardy. Did this come from me saying that it was only appropriate for Dad and me to meet for counseling? If that's so, why would either of you take that as an affront to your relationship?

Mom—even after rereading my letters, you still perceive me as defective and hurting when I've said repeatedly . . . I'm not in pain; my life is better than ever. I'm happy and my friendships are great. I'm managing my finances well, and I've been extremely productive and am taking great pleasure in my work. . . . You don't show me any love or respect—you keep telling me how I feel with no regard for what I've said. . . . It saddens me that you don't see me. . . .

Dad—where did your notion of a clandestine plot come from? . . . To imply I'm crazy to feel how I do and in the next breath tell me that you respect me makes no sense to me. . . .

You haven't asked me why I feel you haven't supported or respected me professionally. If you want to know and respect my feelings, why don't you ask me about them, instead of criticizing my perceptions? I wish you'd stop telling me to get over the past, or discounting my feelings by implying I'm holding a grudge.

I want to get over the past in our relationship, but it takes your acknowledging both the good and the bad with me. Dad . . . your first letters were so good. You . . . responded to my letters and took responsibility for some of what I had said. But your last response was a complete U-turn. It leaves me in the lurch. . . . You seem to be unwilling to work things out with me because Mom can't. . . . I don't see how you and I can work things out without having a relationship that is separate from Mom. I am not indicting your relationship with her—I am saying that it is impossible for her to relate to me.

Love,

Dave

Tension commonly arises when one parent makes an attempt to deal with the confronting letter and the other parent cannot or will not. If Dave's father is able to stay out of the trap of rescuing an unresponsive mate, it can help heal the relationship with his son. This step inevitably breaks a contract with the wife, though, and so may jeopardize the marital relationship. In the above letter (number 11) Dave responds to his parents' defensiveness. His parents jump to the conclusion that Dave is indicting their marriage, although Dave has said nothing about it. Probably, his parents intuitively feel their relationship is in jeopardy if they deal with the truth of what their son is saying about the family dynamics.

If Dave keeps requiring that his dad not cover up his mom's

lack of response, and if he keeps differentiating his parents and not allowing the "we" responses, it is not clear what solution his father will ultimately choose. It very much depends on his dad's motivation and ability to have and to keep a healthy relationship with his son and to deal honestly with the family dynamics. To keep the momentum going, given his wife's inability or unwillingness to respond, will take a great deal of courage and effort on his father's part. But he has already responded with some openness to his son's letters.

It was not until the letters home and the responses they elicited, that Dave, like Susanna (Chapter 6), could fully understand how his mother perpetuates his father's abusive behavior toward him. The response letters clearly reveal to Dave that his mother's love is saccharin, without nourishment. Through the letter dialogues, Dave came to see that what looked like (and she probably meant as) support from his mother in the past undermined his growth. He was not encouraged to stick up for himself with his dad. Instead, he was encouraged to make secret pacts with his mother and to get close to her by allowing his father to victimize him. This family dynamic had trained him to position himself as victim in order to get close to people he cared about and then to leak out his anger in sneaky, passive-aggressive ways.

Dave's father did ask for a joint therapy session. He was willing to visit and come to a two-hour session without his wife. What surprised me was that he was afraid. He had been much more open in the letters than in person. The intimacy of the session made him so insecure that he continually jockeyed for power, trying to dominate me and his son. He said his main task was to listen but he was unable to; he proceeded to lecture, to deny, and to try to make Dave and me as impotent as he felt. The session made it clear that in person, at least in the present, his father has only two available responses to Dave: I abused you terribly and I deeply regret it, but you were my favorite, the best and the brightest and I wanted so much for you, so you are required to forgive me; or I refuse to admit that I intruded, controlled, and invaded you and still do.

In hindsight, the session was probably initiated too early in the process. However, it may also indicate that it is easier and much less frightening for Dave's father to deal with difficult emotional material on paper. Letters provide the built-in distance that Dave's father apparently needs to communicate openly.

The experience with Dave's father opened my eyes to the limits of letter therapy as well as the potential. Because Dave was able to be so open and say everything he wanted to his father, and because his father, for the most part, put great effort into responding to Dave's written confrontations, I was under the illusion that the ground covered in their letters would serve as a jumping-off point for in-person dialogue. And since the letters served to motivate and create the goodwill necessary to bring his father to a joint therapy session, we both had hopes that the session would deepen the communication. My experience prior to that session had been that letter dialogues usually opened up the issues. When the outcome by mail was positive, family therapy sessions or in-person meetings without therapists usually took off from that point and built on the gains accomplished in writing.

It was impressive that his father made the trip without his wife and put the effort into meeting in a therapy situation that was entirely foreign to him. This meant a lot to Dave in spite of the surprise and disappointment we both felt about the unsatisfactory and even torturous session. During the session I tried to go too fast, cover too much ground, and deal with core issues. This was a mistake. On the other hand, the session provided Dave with a witness who saw how difficult his father was to get through to; he got to see me, with all my experience and therapeutic skills, fail to help his father to be open with or even curious about his son. After the session we could brainstorm, because of our shared experience, on how to disengage when his father discounted him, denied his perceptions, and tried to bully him. In addition, Dave developed empathy for his father based on his awareness of his father's fear of real closeness. Surprisingly, Dave reported that the session had a positive after-effect; during the rest of the visit, his father was able to get a little closer to him and to be a little less controlling. It may be that he was so unresponsive during the session because he wasn't on his own turf and felt that the two of us were ganging up on him.

Since the session, Dave has been able to label nonproductive interactions as nonproductive and stop communications with his father when they are in the old, unhealthy mold. He has been more comfortable with his father. The main goal has been accomplished. Dave understands why he has a difficult time asserting what he wants when it is different from what someone else wants. Now that he can differentiate himself from his father, he can more easily differentiate himself from others. He is, for the most part, free of fear of his father and is no longer so upset that his father does not really know or accept him; instead, he is struggling with the reality that ultimately he may not be able to fully accept his father.

After the visit, his father wrote and called Dave. I include some excerpts from Dave's response letter:

12. *Dear Dad,*

After you called last Sunday, I thought about how far we have come, and how much I appreciate that you want to work things out. It meant a lot to me that you wanted to meet for a session. . . .

. . . In the session . . . you didn't seem to listen to what I

had to say, or as you said, know how to. . . . I understand that
you have put most of your energy into being a great surgeon
and that you are behind on relationships. . . . I want you to be
curious about what I am thinking or feeling instead of focus-
ing on how you think I should feel or what I should think. You
were willing and able to do this after our session, and I was im-
pressed with your curiosity. I am willing to change by speaking
up, unlike I have done in the past, and like I did after the
session. . . .

Love,
Dave

Dealing directly with a parent often generalizes to other parent
figures. Around the time Dave wrote the above letter to his father,
he decided to write a letter to the chairman of his dissertation
committee, who had been an academic mentor and friend to
him. Ben's return letter was wise and generous. Following their
open letter exchange, Dave could embrace the wonderful relationship they had without contaminating it with his anger, projections, and perfectionistic expectations:

Dear Ben,

. . . I think I have been mixing criticisms of you and my fa-
ther, and in the process, wiping out much of all you have given
me. I think this was why I was flippant and vague at lunch and
why I dropped out of sight after I left. You reliably responded
by not getting into it with me, and I felt your instinctive dis-
tance.

For me to clear things up, I have to unveil a criticism of you
that I have until now kept hidden. While you have been a
great academic father to me, I have been quietly critical of you
not doing better with your own family. In my own life, my fa-

ther doesn't have the psychological resources that you have (this really sunk in when I had the session with him the day before I saw you). Part of the reason I get caught up in this is because it is difficult for me to see someone so gifted and capable as you be such a good father to me, but not do so in your family life . . . especially when I know you have the abilities to figure this stuff out. . . . It also saddens me because this is something I imagine you wanting more of. You have expressed some regrets along these lines.

What I didn't tell you about the session with my dad was that, while at times horrendous, it was enormously beneficial to me. He was incredibly defensive and unwilling and unable to acknowledge most of what I had to say. His behavior was so controlling that he for the most part impeded Terry's best efforts as a therapist. It was good for me to see the extent of what I have had to deal with. I owe how far I've come to you (and to Terry). . . . I did stand up to him in a way I had never done before, . . . I came away feeling much more differentiated, and unafraid of him.

. . . Since returning to Harvard, I've noticed how it has been easier to value and state my own opinions clearly. . . . I am more aware of a difference in how I respond to authority. . . . I have been more effective and appropriate—very clear without getting so pissed off I don't express myself. . . .

Dave

15

Sideways Writing

CREATIVE APPROACHES

A poem, a cartoon, or a lyric can function as a letter home in that it is written, not spoken, and it is looked at when the creator is not present. When Aaron, my oldest son, was five and six, he would tape cartoons he had drawn and captioned to our bedroom door. They were very funny and at the same time bitingly critical about something I or my husband had done that day which he considered to be unfair. This was Aaron's version of a letter home. Over the years, several of my clients have invented their own formats for their letters home.

Julie's letter to her ex-husband started as an exercise. Just as one letter is sometimes all that is needed to renew a relationship, one good-bye letter is sometimes all that is needed to end a relationship that belongs in the past. Julie picked a man like her deceased father, an intelligent, self-absorbed tyrant, to be her husband. She entered group therapy after several years of psychoanalysis. She had divorced her husband years before, but she still felt plagued by him.

Julie did not intend to break into poetry in her letter, nor did she intend to send the letter. After she wrote it (she reports it just flowed out), she became convinced, with some help from her therapy group, that it would do her good to send it. She did, and it ended her negative connection to Michael. To her amazement, Michael is no longer an issue for her even in grocery stores:

Michael,

Over twenty years of our lives we have spent together, positioned mostly back to back, attached to one another, but only faintly curious about each other. Your needs commanded the field and I hid behind you. Into your shadow I gradually withdrew and withered into oblivion.

Your last words to me jolted me. You said: "We have hurt each other very much." I thought, how strange for you to suggest that I had any impact upon you whatsoever.

From our earliest days you did not require me to feel, think, or act. You wanted me to watch you and so I did: to watch you talking about lofty ideas, looking up, reaching into the air, to watch you pleasuring yourself in your intricate web of thoughts, and to watch you gossip directly into the telephone. We never could talk to each other.

When I conversed with others, you did not like what you overheard. You found it embarrassing and took to ignoring me, sitting right next to me at the dinner table. Other people wondered why you did not pour me wine or why you did not offer me food. I did not. I knew I had ceased to exist.

We connected neither with warmth nor with rage. Your out-

bursts of hate and anger did not touch me. Achtung! the mad-
man—it will pass, keep very still!

Now, ten years later, I brace myself and stiffen when, by
chance, I see you in the grocery store, and often my eyes sweep
along the aisles to check that you're not lurking there. Lurk-
ing? Are you a threat to me, old man, you, bent over your cart
and puttering among your groceries? But no! I will let you
pass, Michael.

> *You're only looking for truffles*
> *to balance the sauce*
> *that tops the cream*
> *that pops the pie.*
> *Goodbye,*
> *Julie*

Tanya wrote out of desperation. She had never spoken of the
feelings expressed in the poem to anyone. It was only after she
had written the poem and the people closest to her had read it
that she could speak freely about those feelings which she had always believed were so heinous as to be unspeakable:

> *I hate the children.*
> *Lucinda and Marcie both have veins close to the skin.*
> *They are beautiful and delicate.*
> *I hate them. I do not want to feed them.*
> *I don't like to keep them busy,*
> *I love to watch them when they are happy.*
> *I do not want to be responsible for them, their happiness,*
> *their minds.*
> *I hate being here. I hate everyone I meet. I hate talking.*

I hate.
How can I get away from here?
I can just leave.
I do not want a car.
I resist planning. I cannot make decisions.
NONE, none none none none none are worth shit.
I could just scream. I do. I scream at the kids.
And hit them.
I guess I wish they were dead and that I was dead.
Or on a beach, or swimming no floating, in salt water.
I strongly dislike the phrase "you are driving me crazy."
I am driving those kids crazy. Kevin doesn't feel the crazy.
Oh, I do wish they weren't here. I wish I were not here.
I can't act. I can't act. I can't react.
I am a great actress. Great, who the fuck do I think I am.

Tanya

In this poem Tanya revealed the extent of her depression and isolation. Although she had been talking around these feelings, the rawness of her poem, which she showed to her husband and later to her group, forced us all to deal head-on with her feelings. She began a course of antidepressants. She talked about her fantasies of escape, including suicide. The shock of this letter stopped her husband from intellectualizing; he began to deal in earnest with the crisis in their marriage and family. Tanya and her husband returned to couples therapy. This time Tanya was significantly more direct about the range and depth of her negative feelings.

....

Larry, the son of biochemists, entered therapy to understand why, in spite of being at the top of his career in science, accomplished, recognized, and wealthy, he felt little pleasure in his career or his marriage or his children. Most of the time he felt deprived, angry, anxious, and depressed. He alternated between vigilance or obsession about the bad things that he expected would happen. He was afraid that he would be abandoned by his wife or that he had contracted AIDS.

During the course of his therapy, he realized how little positive input his father had had in his life. An interaction he had with his father when he was a little boy made an indelible impression on Larry. The interaction seemed emblematic of his father's snatching away his pleasure. Larry realized that now he was the one responsible for taking away his own pleasure. He would no longer allow someone else to snatch away his pleasure from him; he would be in control and do the snatching himself. This poem is his form of a letter home to his dead father.

COAL

I know that you still don't know
What you did to me
When I jumped off the school bus
And ran, leaping, into our house
With a small piece of coal
Which was shiny and beautiful
And cost me a nickel

You stopped me cold
And raged
About the value of coal
Which was nothing

But if I'd had that coal
On the rainy day

When, as your only son,
I picked up that first shovel . . .

I'd've thrown it hard and watched it
Hit and bounce on the pine box
Shiny and black and precious.
To give you a chance
to think about it.

Larry felt immensely relieved to have finally gotten closure on this old, bad memory in a creative way. His poem served somewhat the same function as Mary's letter to her mother had (Chapter 9); Larry became aware that his internalized negative father grew more powerful whenever he experienced pleasure. Having written the poem, he could counter the harmful message that monetary value was the only value. Larry searched for and found a shiny piece of coal that he keeps as a constant reminder to take pleasure in what appeals to him and decide for himself what that is.

16

Inside-out Writing

IF YOU DON'T GET A RESPONSE, INVENT ONE

Carrie had tried over the years to get close to her father. She wrote him, she wrote music for him, she invited him to her concerts, she tried to talk to him, all to no avail. If he responded at all, it was to send her clippings. She knew it would not help to write him because he would not respond. So she decided she would make up his response, what he would have written back if he had written. Writing this imaginary response was her creative way of using letter therapy to make herself fully conscious of what she already knew but was denying. This technique worked so well for her that I have asked others who are in the same predicament to write imaginary responses. The imaginary response helps the writer break out of a conflict with the parent independently of the parent's response or lack of response:

Carrie,

You've asked me to write a letter. You know I'm not the kind who a) writes letters, b) would open up emotionally, and c) would leave a paper trail disclosing any information that might be used against me at a later time.

So this is purely Hypothetical, of course. I want you to understand that I would not take this time with anyone, least of all one of my kids, because none of you share my values. I must state emphatically that this was your idea, and nothing I can be held accountable for. This IS Your Imagination!

Dear Carrie,

K. L. Wood here. Understand you want to hear from me about what I would say to you if I were capable of communicating with you (or anyone) what I feel.

First you must know I don't write letters. Clippings are my specialty—I can stay in touch without revealing anything, and I can feel satisfied that I've done my duty as father. Second, you must also know that you are not a priority in my life. Why do you think I have this catalog of dates and figures in my mind? So I can impress you that I remember your date of birth?? Hell! I'm just trying to determine which one of seven kids I'm talking to! If it weren't for my brilliant idea to name all the girls in alphabetical order, I'd really be lost.

Let's see—Carrie—, starts with "C"—that means you're the third child born. Annie, 1953, Bonnie 1955, Carrie (spelled the way I intended it and not the way your mother misspelled it on your birth certificate)—you were born in 1956. That's right, it was Mother's Day. Oh, gosh darn it anyway! I forgot I was supposed to be at my mother's this afternoon. I should have left a half hour ago if I was going to be on time.

I change the subject when I talk with you because then I get to call the shots and be in control, you know, like Crazy Eights. Say did you know that game was invented by a fellow who grew up in Chicago? Okay, if I can't humor you or charm my way out of this I'll go ahead and get it over with.

1. I never loved your mother.

2. It was a mistake to get married. If only I had had a parent who took an interest in me and my affairs, I might have gotten some counsel about marriage. (That is not to say I would have listened or taken heed necessarily.)

3. My first real love was when your sister Annie was born.

4. I really wanted to have kids, but . . .

5. I lost interest in you all when you started to develop personalities. (Only Ellen will forever remain the star of my life. Not only did her features favor the Stone side of the family . . . but she died as an infant.)

6. I feel absolutely no responsibility for you kids because you don't reflect my values. You are all a product of your mother's values, and it's a damn shame, too.

7. I wasted my time being married to your mother. She took advantage of me. She spent my money—all the money I earned—on things I did not approve of, like private school for you older girls. She nearly broke us. We were all headed for the bottom and it was all her fault!

8. I had great dreams for the family and the farm, but none of you kids took an interest in the farm or my dreams. I couldn't talk to you about these things because your mother wouldn't allow me access to you kids.

You see, Carrie, I am a good man. I had good ideas, good intentions, great dreams. And because of your mother, the Bank of Colorado, the DNR, Mr. Rifkin, not to mention the terrible upbringing I suffered with two parents who didn't care about

*my successes or my troubles, I have not been able to do the
things I would have liked to do. You say I have made my mark
in life by never having anything I couldn't just blow up—walk
away from the rubble and leave the dust to settle in my wake.
It is not lonely out here all by myself, as you might say.*

*I am perfectly content with my life the way it is. No inti-
macy means no responsibility. No one depends on me, and
that's the way I like it. I have freedom. This script is my legacy
to all of my offspring. I gave up long ago trying to have any in-
volvement with you kids because you all adopted your mother's
values.*

*Now to get to the part you are really interested in (and all
you really want from me)—money. Where's your piece of the
pie?*

*You know the story: The land was mine. None of you kids
took an interest in it. Why would you expect to get anything
out of it? I lost the farm in foreclosure, and though I am sad-
dened, I am at least relieved to report to you kids, "Don't come
to me for financial support because I've got nothing to give."
I'm broke. I can be selfish and have the bank to blame it on.*

*I've always suspected that the only time you kids came to me
was when you wanted money. Now I'm convinced of that. And
I will not only make sure you have no inheritance, or any part
of my hard-earned income, but I will destroy any notion you
had about the land being retained in its natural state—agri-
cultural and wetlands preserved as a wildlife refuge. Out of
self-preservation, I must be willing to see the value of that land
for housing development. You kids will not see any of that
profit, I've made sure of it. Twenty years ago I had you all sign
a statement waiving any claim to my business interests at the
company or the land.*

To reiterate: There will be no inheritance! You're lucky

*you had a father who provided for your schooling, shelter, food,
and clothes all those god-awful years I was married to your
mother.*

*Well, this is entirely too much time on a letter. But you are
still unsatisfied? Well, that's the story. No inheritance. No sat-
isfaction. I really don't want to have a relationship with you,
Carrie, or any of your sisters and brothers. It takes too much
time—it's too costly for me. I am content to be a workaholic; I
can justify all of the time I have committed over the years to
keep this business afloat. I won't give up even as we head into
bankruptcy court. I am powerless to change the course of
events set for me as a child, a young married man with too
many children, and a businessman heavily in debt.*

*But I am happy with my life now. I have paid my dues to
you kids and your mother, and I am free of any responsibility to
you. I hope this sets the record straight so you will see my side
of the very biased story you have gotten from your mother. I'm
glad you asked for this letter. Now I think I'll make copies to
send to all your brothers and sisters and be done with you all at
once.*

Good luck in your future,

Dad

When she wrote this letter, Carrie discovered that her father
had something to give her after all. In her imaginary letter from
him, she re-created his straightforward and blunt manner about
what he wanted and what he did not want. He was assertive on
his own behalf. He had no trouble saying no, even if he thought
it would hurt the other person's feelings. Writing this imaginary
letter from her father, Carrie became aware that she could be direct (after all, she wrote the letter with brutal directness, as if she
were her father), and that it could help her tremendously. She

knew through her work in therapy that she often said yes when she meant no to avoid hurting other people's feelings. She knew that when she did this she became angry because she ended up doing what the other person wanted and not what she wanted. She would get back at this person by not keeping her promise, by rejecting them indirectly, and by other passive-aggressive maneuvers. She was already very aware that this behavior hurt the other person more than an original honest "no" would have and hurt her as well by keeping her angry and unfulfilled.

After writing the letter she imagined her father would have written, Carrie stopped trying to get a response from him. More than that, the act of writing this letter completely severed her emotional connection to him. Her letter also helped her disconnect from her former boyfriend. He had been writing her, pleading with her to get back with him at the same time he put her down (what was wrong with her that she broke up with him, she must be very disturbed and unable to receive love, etc.). This kept her feeling bad and mad.

Carrie had written a letter to her boyfriend in which she detailed all her feelings and understanding of how he and she were not good for each other; she had both given and taken responsibility. In his response letter, he ignored everything she said in her letter and asked plaintively why she broke up with him as if she had not just poured her heart out explaining it.

In her new letter to her former boyfriend, she borrowed her father's brutal honesty and said exactly what she thought and felt. It worked:

Dear Sid,
PLEASE STOP! sending letters, poems, and photos of the boys [his boys from his previous marriage]. I do not appreciate your attempts to try to win my affection, or kindle my guilt.

You have said on numerous occasions that you do not want to be in a relationship with someone who is not in love with you. I am not in love with you. Why are you investing so much energy in something that offers No Return?? It is really pitiful, Sid, to see you pouring out your "Heart" as if to win mine in return. Pitiful is Not attractive.

The only purpose these things could serve is to make me feel guilty about leaving you and the boys. As if, out of guilt, I would return? As if a relationship based on guilt and anger is better than no relationship at all. I am not interested.

You imply that when I am ready, there may be an opportunity for a healing to take place. Your message hasn't changed. Somehow I am the one holding up the process, because of some unwillingness I harbor, some unwillingness I have about confronting the Truth. But you've left yourself out of the equation. When you are willing to look at the anger you have toward me and your role in the dysfunction of our relationship, then there might be something we can talk about.

You act like you do not know why I ended the relationship. You are waiting over and over again for me to fill you in. I stated it clearly in the letter I wrote you in the spring of last year. If you really want to know, I suggest you reread that letter. In case the letter was thrown away, I am enclosing a copy.

I do not want to hold onto only the negative aspects of being in a relationship with you, but those are the things I am reminded of when I receive your guru-poetry letters and see your sad-puppy face when I run into you on the street. I urge you to get professional help to take a critical look at your part in wanting to keep this unhappy time of my life/your life alive.

Sincerely,

Carrie

A few months later, she heard that Sid was engaged to be married. This confirmed her perception that instead of caring about her he had been venting his anger by guilt-tripping her. Constructing the imaginary response letter from her father helped her to see that she often picks men who have little to offer her but who initially seem to promise they will pay attention to her and take care of her in ways she longed to have her father take care of her.

PART V

Facing Reality

I wanted to change the world.
But I found out the only thing one can be
sure of changing is oneself.

—ALDOUS HUXLEY

. . . the willingness to accept responsibility for one's life
is the source from which self-respect springs.

—JOAN DIDION

17

Taking Responsibility
for the Rest of Your Life

A total nonresponse is even harder to deal with than threats. The recipient ignores the letter as if the writer had never sent it, hoping that if he or she does not mention the letter, the whole issue will go away. One way of handling this is for the writer to repeat, "I sent you a letter. It is important to me that you respond. If you continue to ignore what is important to me, I will cut off contact with you because this is not good for me."

Family dynamics and pathology become unveiled in the response or lack of response the letter home elicits. It is hard to keep denying what went on in the past when it happens all over again in the present in response to the letter. The response letter becomes a way of reckoning with the past and moving on to a future that is unencumbered with myths about the family.

If the response letter repeatedly makes clear that the recipient does not comprehend what the writer is saying, has not taken the writer seriously, or has ignored everything in the letter that was critical, it is helpful for the writer to send a copy of the original letter with a note saying that the respondent did not "get it" and that the writer expressed himself the way he wanted to the first time so the recipient should reread the original letter and respond to the real content. Too often writers who get this kind of nonresponse response fall into the trap of denying reality by trying harder, restating the same things said in the original letter in a new way. If the writer is tempted to say it all again or teach it or preach it, he needs to reread his original letter. If it is clear, he can just keep sending copies. If he finally gets a decent reading by the recipient, terrific. If he does not, he needs to deal with the reality that the parent is not able or willing to see him or hear him or deal with him. When this happens, it is time to stop hoping. In the words of my sister, Laurel Goldman, in her novel *The Part of Fortune*, "Hope's a thief, he'll rob you blind."

....

Ken continued to get a poor response to his letters. (His other letters to his parents and the poem his parents sent him appear in Chapter 9, and a letter to one of his siblings appears in Chapter 7.) In his own time, he realized that he has difficulty expressing feelings because expression of feelings has been so negatively reinforced by his whole family. Ken's final letter is his way of dealing with this reality:

> *Dear Mom and Dad, Georgia, Jake, and Carl,*
> *I've been reading and rereading your letters. I guess I've been looking for hope, but I've been disappointed. So rather than deal with more defensive denial or your rationalizations for how this is all my problem, I've given up.*
> *It would have been nice to have heard:*

I'm sorry you're so angry.
I'm sorry you feel abandoned.
I'm sorry I know so little about you.

It would have been good to hear you acknowledge your parts in this. But I didn't get any of these things. Instead I got "Don't make waves," "Cover it up," and "This is your problem." So I've given up on you.

I've continued to build a new family for myself with people who know me well and who care enough to ask questions, to be critical, and to let me be critical and to give opinions.

I'm still angry at times, but I find that my anger has propelled me to act and it's not holding me back. I don't think I'll be able to buy into our family myths anymore. I'll not be forever dragging up the past and throwing it in your faces. It's not very productive and it won't change what happened. . . . This doesn't mean that I don't want to hear from you or that I'll be unpleasant to talk to. I'll be as cordial as I ever was. So call if and when you like.

Love,
Ken

One favorable outcome of Ken's final letter home has been the very belated (four years) positive response from his brother Carl. This has helped initiate the first real intimacy Ken has had with any of his family (see Chapter 7). Ken remains in only minimal contact with his parents and other siblings. He no longer feels any obligation to keep up a phony front with them.

If you haven't behaved in a way you can respect, it is hard to hold your parents responsible for what you don't like or don't respect in them. Giving up hope is far easier after you have been honest and open. Even if your parent gives a totally inadequate response, that very inadequacy can help set you free.

....

Ellen was a bright, attractive, shy M.D. who clearly lacked an emotional education. Her mother died when she was young, and she was left with her inadequate, narcissistic father. Because he was all she had, she kept pretending he was a decent father. Because she was caught in this hope/pretense, she married an inadequate, paranoid, and narcissistic man who gave her nothing.

Although she entered therapy with me ostensibly to decide whether she should have a baby at this point in her career and marriage, she was clearly depressed and needing to talk about her awful relationship with her husband. Ellen wanted an outside perspective to see whether the problem was hers or his or theirs. She was not used to talking or thinking about feelings and had little frame of reference for understanding what was going on in her marriage. I referred her husband to individual therapy. He turned out to be incapable of insight. He believed his wife was the cause of all the problems in the marriage and, for that matter, all his problems.

With hard work and adequate time, Ellen faced how terribly destructive her marriage was. She saw the similarity between her husband and her father, and she left her husband. As with Meg (Chapter 4), it was the idea of raising children with her husband and having them feel as miserable as she had that gave Ellen the impetus she needed to leave the marriage.

The following year, after writing many drafts (see Chapter 5), she wrote this letter to her father. She sent a copy with a cover letter to both her sisters and to her brother. Ellen's letter home

ended her relationship with her father and severely altered her
relationship with her older sister Mona:

Dear Dad,

*. . . When I think about my childhood, I don't remember
happy times. I never knew if you would be in a good mood or
a bad mood when you came home, and I remember being
afraid of you coming home because you might be angry. I never
felt like you were happy about anything I ever did. I can't
imagine how I could have done anything more to please you: I
was one of the smartest kids in school. I was good at nearly
everything: math, science, art, languages. I won trophies for
sports. I graduated early and got a scholarship to Yale. Why
don't I have any memories of pleasing you?*

*Instead, I remember when I was very young being scared of
you hitting me. I remember one time I went across the street
to another kid's house where I wasn't supposed to go. I was
brought back across the street and you slapped me on the head.
To this day I have no idea why I wasn't supposed to go there,
but I can still remember how shocked and scared I felt that you
would hit me like that. I also remember threats about being hit
with a belt. I don't think I ever was, but I think that Harry
was. Worrying about being hit with a belt was as bad as actually being hit with one, maybe even worse.*

*I know now that it's not my fault you were so angry. But
when I was a child, I didn't know that, and I thought it was my
fault that you were angry all the time. I felt responsible for
your feelings, and you never did anything to let me know that
I wasn't responsible.*

*The memories of you are memories of a bigot, angry at the
whole world: blacks, women, Jews, Italians, doctors, lawyers,*

politicians, anyone and everyone. I was horrified and embar-
rassed that you could make such awful remarks about people.
You obviously didn't consider children important enough to
care about how we would react to what you said. . . . You were
too cowardly to insult people to their faces, yet we had to hear
your remarks . . . about Italians when Linda was my best friend
in elementary school and about Jews when nearly all my high
school friends were Jewish. They were even nice to you! Stop-
ping by to say, "Hello, Mr. McDougal, how are you?" Little did
they know that you were insulting their parents the night be-
fore. . . . I recall your attitude toward doctors: I know the med-
ical profession has a lot of problems, but the basic idea is to
help people. Your attitude was that doctors are just a bunch of
crooks (like lawyers and politicians), and so I could never feel
like you approved of what I was doing with my life. . . .

*   . . . You never asked me about my life; what I was thinking*
about doing when I finished high school, what interests did I
have, what were my dreams. . . . Our interactions consisted of
me pretending to listen to your raving monologues while actu-
ally watching TV or reading. I would watch the clock, and af-
ter listening for an hour, my duty would be done, and then I
could leave. I waited for the war story (or whatever story) to
reach the point where you saved the day; why did they always
end that way? Wasn't anyone else ever the hero?

*   You and Mom had a miserable relationship. I don't remem-*
ber the two of you ever going anywhere for fun: out to dinner,
to a movie or play. You didn't have any shared interests in any-
thing, nothing to talk about, joke about, laugh about. You
didn't have friends who came to the house . . . no day-to-day
friendships for us to learn from. How do you make friends?
How do you trust people? You taught us not to make friends,
not to trust anyone.

When Mom got sick and needed radiation treatments for a month, I was the one to drive her there every day (I was seventeen and had a learner's permit, so this is my memory of learning how to drive). You should have taken her. You should have been by her side through her illness. I hadn't realized how much you abandoned her until recently when I've taken care of women with breast cancer. The husbands are so supportive of their wives; they arrange a leave from work in order to be with their wives. You were self-employed or unemployed or working odd jobs; you could have been with her. I guess by that point your marriage was so bad that she didn't want you there anyway. It's too bad she couldn't have had another chance with someone who could have loved her. It really makes me angry when you say things about what a wonderful woman she was; why didn't you say that to her when she was alive?

I know now that the reason I put up with such a bad marriage myself is because the example I saw growing up is what I thought I should expect. On the surface my choice looked better: Neil was educated, we did a lot of things together (travel, sports). But he was really just like you: totally self-centered. When it came to the important things . . . Neil was no better for me than you were for Mom. You never treated me or Mom with respect or thoughtfulness or affection, so I didn't look for that in a husband. It was only when I became very depressed and started seeing a therapist that I began to realize that I was putting up with a miserable marriage the same way that Mom did.

While growing up in your house, there was never any talking about anyone's feelings. Even your anger was sometimes expressed as silent hostility (not talking to anyone for days at a time). The children were not allowed to have opinions about anything unless they agreed with yours. Why do you think I

am so quiet? I learned to keep silent so that I wouldn't say any-
thing that might displease anyone. Eventually I learned to
hide my anger completely. . . . I lost all connection with my
true feelings and lived in a numb existence for a very long
time. I married Neil because it felt comfortable to be with a
man who denied my feelings, didn't expect me to have any
opinions, didn't care if I did, got angry at the world for no real
reason, expressed his anger by being sullen and withdrawn,
was not physically affectionate, had no friends, no hobbies, re-
mained emotionally distant (just like you). . . .

I am no longer putting up with the kind of abuse I had to
take when I was a child and depended on you for food and
shelter. I provide my own food and shelter now, and I choose
friends who care about me and treat me with respect. I don't
have time for people who ignore my feelings. I hope you can
answer this letter with something other than denial.

Ellen

cc: Mona, Deena, and Harry

For Ellen, the futility of her struggle with her father became
strikingly apparent when she received his three-sentence response. She finally understood that a pretend father was more
harmful to her than no father. She became very sad, openly sad,
but she was not depressed as she had been before. She knew she
was mourning the loss of what she never had. She wrote the following letter:

Dear Dad,

Your response to my letter is a perfect example of what it is
I'm trying to say: You are not willing to make the effort to have
a relationship with me if it means doing anything difficult. . . .

Instead of facing the facts about how badly we were raised and trying to do something to change the unhealthy patterns, your response is to walk away. In order to justify your behavior to yourself, you pretend you are the victim. You'll just "stay out of the way." You missed the point. You already abandoned me for the first thirty-eight years of my life. I was giving you a chance to change that. I guess now I can stop pretending that I have a father and you can stop pretending that you are one.

Ellen

Ellen did not get a second response from her father. She knows not to expect one. She is dealing with the painful reality that after having been orphaned with an utterly inadequate father, she chose to continue this script with an inadequate and destructive husband. She knows why the marriage was bad, why she stayed so long, and feels terrible regret for wasted time.

Ellen wrote a letter to her older sister in response to her sister's violent reaction to the letter Ellen wrote her father. All her life, Ellen had been unable to disagree openly with her older sister; when there was conflict between them, Ellen stayed invisible. Ellen's letter to Mona shows how secure Ellen is in her differentiation from the family pathology. In this letter, Ellen takes her sister on for the first time in her life. Ellen's letter illustrates how even unsupportive and attacking responses from a sibling (her other sister supported her and her brother stayed neutral) can strengthen the letter writer's resolve rather than undermine it if the writer has support from friends, other siblings, therapy, or all three:

Dear Mona,

I am disappointed to see that you persist in your denial of how badly we were raised. You have shifted your argument:

Now you are attacking my method more than the content of what I am saying. Interesting tactic, but the message is the same; don't rock the boat, shut up and pretend that it really wasn't so bad. There isn't a great deal of logic in your argument. Giving Dad a written copy of my thoughts allows him infinite time for reply, much more than a conversation would. I asked for a written response because I have never been able to have a real conversation with him. Are you forgetting that he is free to say or do whatever he wants (ask questions, discuss topics, tell me his point of view)? . . . He can make his own choices, and frankly his written response was probably as honest as he could be. He did not send me flowery denials about the way we were raised or ask me to pretend it was okay. He essentially confirmed what I had to say by not arguing with it. . . . When confronted, he is incapable of acknowledging his mistakes and having an honest relationship, but at least he doesn't try to fake it.

I understand that right now may not be a good time for you to address personal issues. It is certainly a very painful process. I feel very fortunate that I reached a point in my life where I could safely do the work I needed to catch up in emotional development. It has taken over two years of intensive therapy, and I could only afford to do this because: 1) my career was cruising in the right direction and I could take time and energy away from work, 2) I don't have children to take care of, so I have more free time outside of work, and 3) I make enough money to afford a good therapist. . . .

Why am I doing this? Of course it is for me. I used to hope that I could really get through to Dad and have a relationship that I see other daughters having with their fathers. I thought it was important enough to try. . . . If I had never tried being totally honest with him, I would have gone on feeling frus-

trated in my relationship with him . . . spending time and energy trying to get blood from a stone; meeting his needs with visits and presents . . . ignoring my needs.

What I can feel good about is that I said what I had to say and gave him a chance to respond. He did respond: He is not interested in the kind of relationship I need. . . . There are plenty of people who can provide what I need from relationships, and I am much happier spending my time and efforts on these people. If you are satisfied with your relationship with Dad, by all means go ahead with it; it's just not enough for me.

I don't know why you think I am "stuck" on this. I am the happiest I have ever been. I feel as if my eyes have been opened in the past two years and I have woken up from a deep sleep . . . I am an excellent scientist and physician, and I am interviewing for faculty positions at the top medical schools; I returned to art class and had an exhibit of sculpture last spring; I got certified in scuba diving; I just came back from a week-long backpacking trip in the Alps. Most importantly, I have good friends now and I know how to take better care of myself emotionally. I know how to identify my needs and see that they are met, and I try not to settle for less.

Love,

Ellen

Ellen knows that there is no way she could have successfully confronted her father in person; she would not have been able to relate even a small part of what she wrote in her letters to him. The same is true of her older sister. She may never be as articulate in highly charged emotional situations as she is in letters. Since her last letter to her father, though, she has become increasingly good at expressing her feelings face to face in and out of her therapy group. Ellen continues to use letter writing as a technique whenever she feels stuck with someone. Sometimes she sends the letter and other times she writes a letter just to sort through her feelings.

Writing the most difficult letters of their lives to confront the most important people in their lives makes writing to resolve other conflicts seem comparatively easy. For many like Ellen, it is a tool that, once honed, continues to be put to excellent use.

18

Reality in Black and White

It is not until he receives the response or nonresponse letter that the writer really experiences how difficult it is to finally be authentic to the most significant people in his life, only to be rejected or ignored or to find that the parent is incapable of an authentic response. It is not until he receives either the good or at least not-bad response letter that the writer experiences how difficult it is to face the regret for not having been truthful with his parents sooner. This was true for Dave (Chapter 14), who was able to banish his exaggerated fear of his bully father with his first confrontational letter. This made him feel powerful, but it also made him feel gutless for never having defended himself or his brothers and sister against his father's tyranny.

When it works well, the writer finally gets responded to, acknowledged, vindicated, reaffirmed, apologized to, understood. Old distortions have a chance to dissipate, so that barriers pre-

venting communication and affection are overcome and there is
a chance to create permanent positive change.

Sometimes the barriers come down, but the chance to create
positive change with the parent is only partially realized or realized for only a limited time.

Often the letter home produces a mixed response, with the
balance on the bad side, which nevertheless offers some hope for
further communication. In those cases, with work on both the
writer and recipient's part, the relationship improves. Occasionally there is great improvement in the relationship with one parent but the other parent will not budge, as was true in Dave's
case.

Too often the writer, like Cindy (Chapter 10), gets the same
negative response to the feelings she expresses that she has always gotten; when this happens, the writer has a strong validation
of her memory and perceptions. Some responses are even worse
than predicted. One letter writer received a response to his letter
to his mother (not included in *Letters Home*) in which his mother
reminded him that his brother before him had gone against her in
the same way. Given that his brother had died years earlier in an
auto accident that looked suspiciously like suicide, this was a
clear death threat.

It is not uncommon for parents or siblings to imply that the letter home caused illness or death. Although none of my clients'
parents died as a result of letters they received, several of Dean's
siblings blamed Dean's letters (Chapter 9) for his eighty-four-
year-old father's death, in spite of his father's previous heart attacks and an array of other health problems. Several writers have
had response notes from their mothers saying that their fathers
have been diagnosed with prostate cancer. The implication is that
the letter home had instantly and magically caused the cancer

and the writer should beware of communicating further painful truths.

The letter writer who finally reveals secrets or tells the truth may easily interpret a poor response to her efforts as being deserved because she was bad for having been angry, critical, or even just assertive. The letter can act as a check on distortion. This was true for Laurie, who had become increasingly aware in her therapy that she gravitated toward men who would ultimately belittle her.

Laurie's letter was the last of three drafts. She had included many "take-aways" in her earlier versions because she was afraid that if she were really honest her parents would cut her off irrevocably or they would die as the result of having to face what bad parents they had been:

Dear Mom and Dad,

I've been feeling angry and sad about things that happened when I was a kid, and want to tell you about them. I hope you will listen with an open heart and mind. . . .

Mom, you squirted us with a water bottle if we put our elbows on the table during dinner. This is how you train an animal, not teach a child. We had to drink standing up for several days if we spilled our milk. We weren't allowed to be children and couldn't relax in our home. We had to be vigilant not to break your arbitrary and unreasonable rules.

Dad, you belittled us when we spoke imprecisely or passionately (e.g. say "tissues" not "Kleenex," say "aluminum foil" not "tin foil"; I was always told I laugh too much, I smile too much, I talk too fast and loud). We had to eat things we didn't like, and we couldn't choose our own clothes. We weren't free to develop and express our own preferences. If we tried to as-

sert our food desires . . . we had to sit at the table until we forced food down. . . . Dad, you didn't allow us to use our house as a home. You collected things we left in any area of the house except our bedroom and made us pay to get them back. And if we didn't have the money to pay for them, we couldn't get our things back, even if we needed them for school. You made us pay for our own abuse. We couldn't play because you called this "making noise" and interfering with your studying. Your needs came first and ours were ignored. At the end of the day after . . . having to sit with our stomach in knots during dinner, we were required to play games, where we were supposed to be having "fun." Instead, Dad, you were enraged and terrifying when you lost. And then you were critical and belittling if we lost. You made "fun" dangerous.

Mom, you told me many times how much you loved me for being your "little ray of sunshine." You did not want me to show my feelings of sadness and anger. I remember coming home from school one day and you were sobbing in your bedroom with the curtains drawn because I hadn't told you I loved you before I went to school. You required me to express love and provide protection. When I was in high school I tried to communicate how angry I was at Dad, and you told me I had to love him because he was my father.

. . . Mom, I vividly remember coming home one Christmas a few years ago, and we stopped at the hospital so you could visit a woman who was dying. I was incredibly touched and moved at how real you were with her, and how you were helping her deal with her feelings of terror and grief about dying. That moment is etched in my memory, as I saw how wonderful you could be at helping someone deal with extremely painful feelings. I was sad seeing this because you have not been real with me, and did not help me deal with my feelings. . . .

Mom and Dad, you promoted an atmosphere of competi-
tion that got in the way of my relationships with Ted and Ella.
I remember being asked to read Swiss Family Robinson *to Ted*
when I was six and he was seven, which was intended to prove
how "smart" I was and how "dumb" he was. And I remember
you putting me down about how I looked and making com-
ments about how pretty Ella was. It left me . . . in a hostile
relationship with Ted and Ella. . . . I participated in this
because I also came away feeling greatly valued for being
smart and for achieving. In a climate of competition and
criticism, it was important to me to feel . . . I could "win" at
something.

I haven't remembered or been able to talk about these things
before. I have to now because not talking about them is a way
of pretending they didn't happen, or that they didn't mat-
ter. . . . You asked me to be fake, to hide real feelings, to be on
my guard. I lived in a climate of coercion and didn't feel safe
and came away from this believing my feelings and thoughts
didn't matter. . . . My ex-husband . . . was overtly reliable, de-
pendable, and safe. But covertly, he was angry at who I was
and controlling and rejecting in the same manner I experi-
enced from you when I was a child.

. . . I have to say these things for myself in order to move
ahead with my life. . . . If you pray, pray for yourselves, not me.
Laurie

The written response is a piece of reality captured in black and
white. When Laurie got her parents' condescending and defensive response letter, she came to the conclusion that she must
have come across as mean in her letter. She reread her letter. She
reread her parents' response letter. She showed it to her therapy
group and friends and took in their reactions. Distortion is diffi-

cult to maintain when the writer can look at the reality in front of her. Clear that her first letter was not mean-spirited, Laurie wrote another letter:

> *Dad,*
>
> *. . . Your reply, or I should say, nonreply, to my letter is why I'm so angry at you. You didn't respond to anything I said. By saying I should continue to get things off my chest, you suggest that the real problem is my emotionality and not my experiences with you and with Mom. I already blame myself too much for what happened.*
>
> *I don't want to be blamed, directly or indirectly, for being angry and hurt. I also don't want to blame you.*
>
> *What I tried to say before, and you didn't respond to, is that you hurt me. . . . You did not tell me what you think, whether you think I'm overreacting, whether you feel you are unjustly characterized, or if you think what you did was wrong, but feel too bad about it to take responsibility for it. Instead, you told me you had cancer and didn't give me any of the details to know how bad it was, leaving me to guess and worry.*
>
> *This angers me. I got information to understand as best I could about skin cancer.*
>
> *If you want to talk—to really talk—let me know.*
>
> *Your daughter,*
Laurie

Laurie's parents have not been able to respond adequately. She no longer feels so angry or entangled with either of them and maintains superficial but friendly contact. In her romantic relationships, she is less likely to believe that she deserves to be belittled and no longer puts up with condescension from others.

At times the writer is so convinced that the significant other is a bad parent, the enemy, that he misreads a good response as bad. For example, Allen's father and sister took his letters home (Chapter 7) seriously; they grappled with what he had said. But by focusing on the few critical points they had made in their responses, he missed the overall openness and generosity of their letters—what I call snatching defeat from the jaws of victory. When his group pointed out his distortions, he could see that he had taken basically good, open responses and acted as if they were the bad responses he had expected. Feedback, whether it comes from a therapy group or a friend, is always crucial. In this case the feedback Allen got prevented him from responding poorly to his father's and sister's openness. (His mother's response was very defensive and he labeled that correctly. He remained in a letter dialogue with her but became increasingly frustrated by her poor response. It was not until they talked in a therapy session that his mother saw how defensive she had been and really opened up to her son.)

Conversely, a writer may be so caught up in hope that he misreads a bad, albeit seductive and tricky, response as good. Dave's first reaction to a particularly flattering letter from his mother (discussed in Chapter 14) is an example. In either Allen's or Dave's case, had there been a person-to-person talk, there would have been no chance of correcting misinterpretations. Having a concrete document allows an outside person to give input that may bring a new perspective. Or rereading the response letter, after putting it aside for a while, the writer can see things on his own that he could not have seen or felt at the height of his emotions. The response letter, because it too is a concrete document, provides perspective in the same way the original letter did.

Whatever the response or nonresponse, the letter writer is forever catapulted out of the realm of fantasy or hope and into reality. With reality as ground, the writer can come to understand himself and his parents; with this understanding he can work to change his pattern of relating to significant others.

Bob Vaillancourt, my cotherapist, brings a religious perspective to our work that I, raised as an ethnic Jew by agnostic parents, do not have. Bob, a lapsed Catholic, was a monk before he became a social worker and my cotherapist:

> The idea of witnessing in the Christian sense of the word is to make public, to testify, to show forth what you hold to be true internally. Witnessing is a powerful concept not only in furthering one's belief system but also in driving home to that person the concreteness, the reality, of what in the privacy of feeling or thought he says he believes. To write a letter home is to witness or make concrete a psychological step forward. The response letter from the parent serves as a clear and visible "witnessing" of the family dynamics. Because it is on paper, the therapist is not required to sort out the client's distortions—that is, those distortions that serve to shield the client from seeing the parent as being as bad as he is as well as those distortions that present the parent as worse than he is.

If the writer is stuck, hung up with her parents or with myths about herself or them, the act of writing a letter can help her get unstuck. As Vaillancourt puts it, the writing itself is a psychological step forward. When the writer contemplates sending the letter, she becomes aware of her fears of the outcome. And when she sends it and finally gets a response or nonresponse, she is forced to deal with the actual as opposed to the imagined outcome—to deal with reality.

When parents are unable to be honest with their children—to speak and show their own feelings, good and bad—this inability inevitably gets repeated in the next generation, spawning masked, inauthentic adults. But when parents are able to be honest with their feelings and allow their children to do the same, this too gets repeated. The writers in this book spoke out in their letters. They changed themselves, and in many cases, these changes are already being passed on to the next generation.

....

Rosie, the ten-year-old daughter of Meg (Chapter 4), is living proof. Meg was sitting in her den when the following note descended from a piece of string:

> *Dear Mom,*
> *I am really mad at you. Here's why, #1. You said you would play with me after dinner, you don't. #2. You never asked what happened when Amy and I got in a fight. So, as of right now I really, truly, honstly, and oh yes, serously hate, despice, and never want to talk to you again.*
> *You're on my last nerve. Your Enemy and daughter,*
> *Rosie Landon Dade*

Meg's ex-husband, like her parents, discourages his children from speaking out, especially if they are expressing criticism or anger, so she took this note as her victory as well as Rosie's. After she read the note, Meg told her daughter how happy she was that Rosie let her know what she was thinking and feeling so that they had a chance to work it out together, which they did in short order.

Each of the writers whose letters appear in *Letters Home* have written to the people they found most important yet most difficult to confront. Because the majority of the writers have experienced profound changes in their lives and at the least have experienced relief from a particular conflict, every letter writer represented here has gone on to use letters to work out conflicts with friends, lovers, spouses, in-laws, teachers, bosses, doctors, even book editors. Many of the writers who went through half a dozen or more drafts of their letters home are now so skilled that they don't need to go through the process of rewriting. They say what they want to say honestly and without defensive "take-aways." Like any other skill, confrontational letter writing gets easier with practice.

The writers represented here faced their pasts and their parents. The process of writing and revising their letters and analyzing the response letters helped them confront their own defenses. Expressing their feelings and thoughts in detail brought relief, and clarity, and closure.

By revealing what was in their minds and hearts, they came to see what they had lost by appeasing and hiding. They used letters home to resolve longstanding conflicts that had kept them imprisoned. Out of prison, they took control of their lives, holding themselves responsible for what was their responsibility and letting go of what was not their responsibility. The letter-writing process helped them learn what they did to perpetuate their problems, and this knowledge gave them the power to continue to change. When the writers began the process of writing home, they could not have imagined that their letters would change their lives and that the impact of these changes would be felt in future generations.

Epilogue

HOW TO READ AND RESPOND
TO A LETTER HOME

It is very difficult to read an angry letter that comes at you out of the blue with what seems to be unfair criticism. It may be especially hurtful when it is written by your grown children because of the role reversal implied, but a confrontational letter from anyone significant to you can feel devastating. It is easy to forget that no matter how confrontational the writer is, it is likely that he is writing to you, at least in part, because he wants things to be better between you. If the writer does not tell you about his anger, grudges, resentments, and secrets, there is no chance to improve your relationship. The writer has initiated an opportunity for both of you to clear up old impasses, but this opportunity can be quickly squandered, setting the problems you've had between you in cement.

The writer undoubtedly put a lot of work into writing to you, and you will need to put a lot of work into your response. It will probably take several drafts. First, read the letter noticing what makes you the angriest, saddest, most defensive—in other words, those statements calling forth the most feeling. It is important not to avoid the feelings the letter evokes. Sometimes it helps to make copies of the letter and write your first reactions line by line on the copy. These will include some defensive responses like:

"That's not what happened! You misunderstood me."

"I was too depressed and preoccupied that day to know what I was doing."

The next step is to write an angry, self-righteous, how-dare-you draft. It will probably include some of your first defensive reactions as well as other statements like:

"You've distorted everything."

"I knew your therapy would ruin our relationship—everything always gets blamed on the parents."

"You unappreciative bitch!"

"How dare you talk to me this way!"

"We did the best we could under very difficult circumstances."

"You're always angry about something. Can't you just forgive and forget?"

"I don't see how this is my fault."

"We've given you so much more than we ever got from our parents."

"Give me a break!"

At this point it is useful to send a note to the writer saying that you received her letter, that you are waiting to get over your initial reaction before you write back, and that you are taking her letter seriously. This eliminates any pressure you may be feeling to respond hastily.

Now put away both the letter home with your first reactions on it and your how-dare-you draft. When you are ready, reread the letter, trying to understand the writer's point of view and feelings. It helps if you can remember times when you had some of the same feelings the writer is describing. For instance, if the writer describes feeling humiliated by you, try to think of a time you felt humiliated by someone. Remember this event in as much detail as you can, write it down, and put it aside. This exercise will help you empathize with the writer.

If you find yourself concentrating on the writer's technique, style, or timing in bringing up her points, you are picking apart the wrapping and avoiding the package. You may, for instance, focus on the writer's bad timing: "You picked the worst possible time to dump this on me." This is a common form of respondent "take-away." It is a very sophisticated and tempting defense because it is easy to find a detail that the writer got wrong or something in the delivery with which you can legitimately find fault. You can then ignore the writer's valid points, which are much more difficult to dismiss than the trivia to which you are choosing to respond. If you send a response letter that reacts to the "wrapping," you will succeed in making the writer defensive and you will get her off track. You will have undermined your chance to be honestly responsive and thus the opportunity to repair the relationship.

Give yourself time. It is hard to get beyond your defenses, even when you are very motivated, because it is so easy to come up with what seem like solid reasons why you are right and the letter writer is wrong. It is critical to analyze your defensive responses once you have them down in black and white. Get help from someone you trust to be honest with you before you write the next draft of your response. Don't be surprised when the person you go to for support and help takes the writer's side and gives you additional unwanted critical feedback. Often I have gone to my husband and sister expecting them to agree that one of my sons' criticisms of me is outrageous, and instead they agree with the gist of what my son has said. I, of course, feel betrayed and am mad at these second "misguided" messengers. When I've had some time to reflect, my husband and sister become valuable teachers, helping me understand what my son means. They are able to get through my defenses because they are not angry at me and are very motivated since, not surprisingly, they have similar issues with me and certainly want me and my kids to have a good relationship. They have the additional advantage of seeing where my sons might be at fault and so can offer support for some of my perceptions as well.

The letter you receive may accuse you of behavior (intentional or not) that you are not proud of, behavior that has been harmful or destructive to the writer. I believe that the worst parenting comes not from the original parental sin, even if that behavior is very bad or abusive. The worst parenting comes from the parents' denial that the behavior happened and/or from their explicit or implicit request that the child keep the parents' bad act secret. The same holds true for any relationship. To deny another's perception of what you know to be true is a violation that inevitably has disastrous consequences. So if you feel defensive because the letter hits the mark, you have a chance to rectify a great deal of past harm by taking responsibility for your actions and thereby validating your friend's or spouse's or son's or daughter's perceptions. Like the writer, you can change for the better first by acknowledging to yourself and then to the writer what you have done that is your responsibility. But just as the writer of the letter home must not take responsibility for behavior that is not the writer's responsibility, you too must sift through the accusations and not take responsibility for what is not your responsibility.

The stages you go through to write your response, like the stages the writer went through before he sent his letter, can offer an opportunity for growth, insight, and change. For you, as for the letter writers included in this book, the change begins even before you drop the letter into the mailbox. Writing an open, non-defensive response is well worth the effort for many of the same reasons it is worth writing letters home.

When you are ready to write the final response, start with what you want to happen as a result of your response. (Reread Chapter 11; much of it applies.) Follow this with a statement of what you understand the writer to be saying and feeling, what you acknowledge of his criticisms, and how you feel about them. Apologize if and only if you feel genuinely sorry. This is not the time for dishonesty. If you find yourself acknowledging in one sentence and saying "but" in the next, you will know that this is still a draft; the "but's" need to be edited out. If there are accusations or criticisms in the letter home that you genuinely believe to be untrue, say so and tell the letter writer what you believe to be true. Give your version, but be aware that this is also an approximation of the truth. Invite the writer's reactions, disagreements, corrections, and additions to your version. This is what a letter dialogue is all about.

Wait a few days before you look at your letter again. Make sure you have responded to each point the writer has made. Edit out any defensive statements. When you don't understand something the writer said in her letter, ask her (in your letter) whatever questions you need answered so that you can respond to her concerns. Put your response letter away. In a few days, reread the letter home and your response. Have your confidante look over your letter and ask her to discuss with you what in your response would put her off and why. Argue with her. If you don't get her point but feel she has one, wait until you do understand her before you revise your letter. When you read your final letter and are proud of it—that is, when it feels true and expresses what you want to say—send it. You are now in a position to understand the hard work the writer went through writing drafts, weeding them out, and rewriting to get to the core of what she wanted to say.

Even in the rare cases when the writer is writing you off, there is still a chance that you may be able to stay in his life, building on his desire to communicate to you. If you respond honestly and openly to his criticisms, you may change yourself and the relationship in the bargain. In the worst-case scenario, you will know why you are being eliminated from his life and can make use of this information even if the relationship is irrevocably over. When the letter writer writes with the sincere intent to improve your relationship, the hard work you have done to respond to him will make a profound change in you and in the relationship between you and the writer of the letter home.

NOTES

....

1. *Benefiting from the Ease and Safety that Writing Allows*

1. J. W. Pennebaker and J. R. Sussman, "Disclosure of Traumas and Psychosomatic Processes," *Social Science and Medicine* 26 (1988): 327–332. See Chapter 2, note 4, for discussion.

   I want to thank Kay Lovelace, who walked into my office one day and handed me two reprints of journal articles by J. Pennebaker. She knew I used letter-writing assignments in therapy and thought that I would find the articles interesting. She didn't know that I had just finished the first draft of *Letters Home*. I was delighted. Here was research confirming what I knew through my clinical practice. Thanks also to my son Aaron, a psychology graduate student at the University of Pennsylvania at the time, who acted as my research assistant.

2. Thich Nhat Hanh, "Hope as an Obstacle," in *Peace Is Every Step* (New York: Bantam Books, 1991), pp. 41–42. Thich Nhat Hanh discusses this destructive aspect of unjustified hope:

   > Hope is important, because it can make the present moment less difficult to bear. If we believe that tomorrow will be better, we can bear a hardship today. But that is the most that hope can do for us—to make some hardship lighter. When I think deeply about the nature of hope, I see something tragic. Since we cling to our hope in the future, we do not focus our energies and capabilities on the present moment. We use hope to believe something better will happen in the future, that we will arrive at peace, or the Kingdom of God. Hope becomes a kind of obsta-

cle . . . and if you dwell in the energy of hope, you will not bring yourself back entirely into the present moment. If you re-channel those energies into being aware of what is going on in the present moment, you will be able to make a breakthrough.

3. P. Greenacre, "Play in Relation to Creative Imagination," *Psycho-analytic Study of the Child* (1959): Monograph 14, pp. 62–78.
4. E. H. Erikson, *Childhood and Society* (New York: Norton, 1963), p. 220; and Terry Vance, "Pretense Behavior and Change: Effects of Responsibility and Irresponsibility on Change Following Positive and Negative Discrepant Role Play" (Ph.D. dissertation, Duke University, 1970).
5. Jacob Moreno, the inventor of psychodrama, maintained that psychodramatic exercises indirectly stimulate the mind toward certain emotional states, all the while working in the safety that pretending provides. See Jacob Moreno, *Who Shall Survive?* (New York: Beacon House, 1953); *Psychodrama* (New York: Beacon House, 1959); "Role Theory and the Emergence of the Self," *Group Psychotherapy* 15 (1962): 4–117; "The Role Concept," *American Journal of Psychiatry* 118 (1961): 518–523.

   George Kelly developed an entire theory and practice of therapy, "fixed role-play therapy," based on the idea that creating safety will promote fast and lasting change. See George Kelly, *The Psychology of Personal Constructs,* vol. I (New York: Norton, 1955), p. 373. Albert Pesso further developed these ideas, creating what he calls PSP, a kind of psychomotor therapy. See A. Pesso, *Moving Psychotherapy: Theory and Application of Pesso System/Psychomotor Therapy* (Cambridge: Brookline Books, 1991); *Experience in Action: A Psychomotor Psychology* (New York: New York University Press, 1973); and *Movement in Psychotherapy: Psychomotor Technique and Training* (New York: New York University Press, 1969). What the techniques of Moreno, Pesso, and Kelly have in common is the safety provided by their make-believe character.
6. Neuropeptides, molecules that act as messengers traveling throughout the body, are considered the biochemicals of emotions and can be measured. For example, a particular peptide is associated with euphoria. See Candace Pert, "Chemical Communicators," in Bill Moyers, *Healing and the Mind* (New York: Doubleday, 1993), p. 187.

See also Margaret Kemeny, "Emotions and the Immune System," in
Bill Moyers, *Healing and the Mind*, pp. 195–211:

> We found that during the intense sad state there was an increase
> in the number of natural killer cells in the actor's bloodstream,
> and that these killer cells were functioning more efficiently than
> they were when the actor was in a neutral state. . . . We found
> that the effect of the happy state on the immune system was very
> similar to what we had seen as a result of the sad state. . . . The
> data suggest that when we experience any emotion, there may be
> similar effects on the immune system, including increases in the
> number and activity of certain cells circulating in the blood-
> stream. . . . We saw an increase in killer cells within twenty min-
> utes. . . . So there was a very brief increase in the number of
> these cells, and then they returned right back to baseline after
> the actor stopped experiencing the emotional state. . . . It's pos-
> sible that the experience of feelings per se, whether they're
> happy or sad, is healthy psychologically and may even be healthy
> physiologically. . . . Natural killer cell activity increased with
> both positive and negative emotional states. One possible con-
> clusion is that experiencing feelings, even negative feelings, has
> a positive impact on natural killer-cell activity. . . . If you're talk-
> ing about the ability to control these states and therefore our
> physiology, I would point to group therapy as an example of a
> psychotherapeutic technique designed to help individuals expe-
> rience feelings more freely. The tendency to suppress feelings is
> psychologically detrimental.

Kemeny compares the adaptive physiological consequences
when we experience emotions to the state of depression, in which
we do not experience emotions fully in response to our environment. According to Kemeny, there are accumulating data that
chronic depression has negative biological as well as psychological
consequences. Recent research dramatically illustrates that even at
a physiological level, a person is remarkably fluid: "People with multiple personalities sometimes have extremely clear physical symptoms that vary with each personality. One personality can be allergic
to cats while another is not. One personality can be diabetic and an-

other not. . . . You can measure it. You can show that one personality is making as much insulin as it needs, and that the next one, who shows up half an hour later, can't make insulin." (Pert, "Chemical Communicators," p. 182.)

For related research in this area, see G. P. Chrousos and P. W. Gold, "The Concepts of Stress and Stress System Disorders," *Journal of the American Medical Association* 267 (1992): 1244–1252; and M. Stein, A. H. Miller, and R. L. Trestman, "Depression, the Immune System, and Health and Illness: Findings in Search of Meaning," *Archives of General Psychiatry* 48 (1991): 171–177.

7. George Kelly elaborates on this idea in *The Psychology of Personal Constructs*, p. 372: "This is probably man's oldest protective screen for reaching out into the unknown. The test tube and the scientific lab are outgrowths of this cautious approach to life. They enable man to explore his world without wholly and irrevocably committing himself."

2. Letters to Confront Problems

1. As Kelly expresses it, once a person has "changed" by virtue of an experiment such as role-play (or writing a letter), she is more likely to be able to say "I can change." See George Kelly, *The Psychology of Personal Constructs* (New York: Norton, 1955).

2. Pennebaker had subjects disclose (in writing) important feelings and events that the subjects knew would never be revealed. In Pennebaker's popular book based on his research, *Opening Up* (New York: Avon Books, 1990), he discusses in some detail his theory of inhibition versus confrontation:

> Active inhibition means that people must consciously restrain, hold back, or in some way exert effort to not think, feel or behave. . . . Inhibition affects short-term biological changes and long-term health. In the short run, inhibition is reflected by immediate biological changes, such as increased perspiration. . . . Over time, the work of inhibition serves as a cumulative stressor on the body, increasing the probability of illness and other stress-related physical and psychological problems. Active inhibition . . . [is] one of many general stressors that affect the mind and body (p. 21).

When a disclosing letter is actually sent to the significant other, it goes one important step further than Pennebaker's subjects went.

3. J. W. Pennebaker, J. K. Kiecolt-Glaser, and R. Glaser, "Disclosure of Trauma and Immune Function Health Implications for Psychotherapy," *Journal of Consulting and Clinical Psychology* 56 (1988): 239–245.

4. J. W. Pennebaker and J. R. Sussman, "Disclosure of Traumas and Psychosomatic Processes," *Social Science and Medicine* 26 (1988): 327–332. Pennebaker contrasts the inhibition of thoughts and feelings associated with an important event to confrontation, by which he means "actively thinking and/or talking about significant experiences as well as acknowledging their emotions" (*Opening Up*, p. 21). Pennebaker's conclusions tally with what our letter writers discovered: that confrontation forces understanding and assimilating and increases emotional and physical well-being:

> Psychologically [by this he means emotionally] confronting traumas overcomes the effects of inhibition both physiologically and cognitively . . . those with the most health problems had experienced at least one childhood trauma that they had not confided. Of two hundred respondents, the sixty-five people with an undisclosed childhood trauma were more likely to have been diagnosed with virtually every major and minor health problem that we asked about: cancer, high blood pressure, ulcers, flu, headaches, even earaches. Oddly, it made no difference what the particular trauma had been. The only distinguishing feature was that the trauma had not been talked about to others. . . . Overall, childhood traumas influence adults' health to a greater degree than traumatic experiences that have occurred in the last three years (*Opening Up*, pp. 21, 30).

Pennebaker would explain a letter writer's healthy changes (even when the letter is not sent) as the result of his having come to a new understanding of events that were formerly overwhelming, thereby producing a reduction in unhealthy stress. See *Opening Up*, pp. 101–104.

Candace Pert, at Rutgers University, discovered peptide receptors in the brain and the rest of the body. Her research enlarges our knowledge of the physical, biological basis for the effect of emotions on health. Pert discusses the effect that repressing emotion has on causing disease and notes that in native cultures healing practices emphasize the release of emotion. In an interview with Bill Moyers for his PBS series and book, *Healing and the Mind*, Pert gives a simplified version of her research and thinking:

> It leads us to think that the chemicals that are running our body and our brain are the same chemicals that are involved in emotion. And that says to me that we'd better seriously entertain theories about the role of emotions and emotional suppression in disease, and that we'd better pay more attention to emotions with respect to health. . . . Positive thinking is interesting, but if it denies the truth, I can't believe that would be anything except bad . . . there is a growing body of literature . . . that suggests that emotional history is extremely important in things like incidence of cancer. For example, it appears that suppression of grief, and suppression of anger, in particular, is associated with an increased incidence of breast cancer in women. (Candace Pert, "The Chemical Communicators," in Bill Moyers, *Healing and the Mind* [New York: Doubleday, 1993], pp. 191–193.)

Other research articles related to this topic include: J. K. Kiecolt-Glaser and R. Glaser, "Psychoneuroimmunology: Can Psychological Interventions Modulate Immunity?" *Journal of Consulting and Clinical Psychology* 60 (1992): 569–575; and J. K. Kiecolt-Glaser and R. Glaser, "Stress and the Immune System: Human Studies," in A. Tasman and M. B. Riba, *Annual Review of Psychiatry* 11 (1991): 169–180.

5. Pennebaker, Kiecolt-Glaser, and Glaser, "Disclosure of Trauma," pp. 239–245.
6. D. Spiegel, J. Bloom, H. Kraemer, and E. Gottheil, "Effect of Psychosocial Treatment on Survival of Patients with Metastatic Breast Cancer," *Lancet* 8668, no. 2 (October 14, 1989): 889–891.

3. Changing the Pattern

1. Eric Berne coined the term "script." For discussion of this term see E. Berne, *Transactional Analysis in Psychotherapy* (New York: Grove

Press, 1961); and E. Berne, *The Games People Play* (New York: Grove Press, 1964).

2. For discussion of "repetition compulsion" see Sigmund Freud, "Beyond the Pleasure Principle," in E. Rickman, ed., *A General Selection from the Works of Sigmund Freud* (New York: Anchor Press, 1957), and Sigmund Freud, "The Relation of the Poet to Day-Dreaming," in *On Creativity and the Unconscious* (New York: Harper, 1958), pp. 44–53.

3. There is a mastery aspect to the notion of repetition compulsion. It was this aspect that the psychologist Erikson emphasized: "the ego's need to master the various areas of life and especially those in which the individual finds his self, his body, and his social role wanting and trailing." E. H. Erikson, *Childhood and Society* (New York: Norton, 1963), p. 212.

5. Writing Drafts and Getting Feedback

1. Ronald Batson, "Multiple Personality Disorder: Conceptual Therapeutic Resolutions," *Highland Highlights* 15, (1992): 5 (from a talk given at the Duke/Highland Conference on Treatment of Multiple Personality Disorder).

10. Pacing the Letters and Deciphering the Responses

1. Additional thanks to Bob Vaillancourt for introducing me to Bishop John Shelby Spong's book, *Rescuing the Bible from Fundamentalism: A Bishop Rethinks the Meaning of Scripture* (San Francisco: Harper, 1991). Spong's view of the origin of fundamentalism and of Saint Paul's beliefs is especially relevant to an understanding of the use to which fundamentalism is put in abusive families. Literal interpretations of the Bible, Spong contends, are often used to justify prejudice and to deny human rights. This is how Saint Paul's teachings were used by Cindy's fundamentalist parents. Spong's theory on the origins of Paul's beliefs is particularly interesting. Cindy's parents quoted Saint Paul to her with a motivation that was probably very

close to Saint Paul's: to deny and try to control his own perception of himself as a secret sinner. Spong contends that Saint Paul loathed himself because of his homosexual desires:

> Paul was never far from the discussion of sexual passion and the need for self-control. . . . Powerful emotional commitments to a controlling religious system reveal not so much devotion and virtue but troubled waters that will not stay calm. . . . It is not surprising to me that . . . the popular evangelistic preachers who speak so vehemently against the sins of the flesh wind up succumbing to the very fleshy sins they have condemned (p. 112).

Cindy came to understand that defending against one's own inner impulses by routing out and condemning those around you was a family tradition. She realized that telling oneself that it is bad to pay attention to your desires, understanding, and feelings is not healthy or normal. During the process of writing letters home, she began to understand how she used Saint Paul's teachings and other Biblical quotations to deny her own feelings and perceptions and to deny as well the secret knowledge that she was not supposed to have about her father's affairs and his alcoholism. In Cindy's family, religion was used as a controlling, pious mask that allowed the entire family to dissociate from their feelings and from reality.

2. According to many neuropsychologists, people's earliest memories do not date back before the age of three to four years, when the storage regions for long-term memory develop. These neuropsychologists contend that declarative memory—that is, memory for facts and events—as opposed to nondeclarative memory—that is, skills and habits—is not developed in children before the age of about three and a half. The current thinking is that declarative memory is necessary in order for information to transfer from short-term to long-term memory. See S. Zola-Morgan, "Memory for Health Professionals," 1993: seminar; unpublished handout summarizing recent research.

Daniel Schacter, professor of psychology at Harvard, has been researching the nature of memory for years and has written a book based on his research, *Searching for Memory: The Brain, the Mind, and the Past* (New York: Basic Books, 1996). How memory is organized and exactly what physiological changes account for memory is still the subject of research. Schacter does discuss the controversy over "recovered memories," but as he acknowledges, we still do not have the definitive answers from psychology or neuropsychology that would allow us to determine the accuracy of a particular memory. As many of the letter writers discovered, the best reality test is often in the current interaction.

3. For further understanding of the debate related to memories of abuse read: N. Wartik, "Memories of Sexual Abuse, Are They Real, A Question of Abuse," *American Health,* May 1993; S. Roan, "Repressed Memory Syndrome Ignites Debate among Mental Health Experts, Memory or Malice," *Raleigh News and Observer,* September 2, 1993; Laura Shapiro, Debra Rosenberg, John F. Lauerman, and Robin Sparkman, "Child Abuse, Rush to Judgment," *Newsweek,* April 19, 1993; L. Wright, "Remembering Satan," *The New Yorker,* 3 parts: May 17, 24, 31, 1993; C. Tavris, "Beware the Incest-Survivor Machine," *The New York Times Book Review,* January 3, 1993; W. Reich, "The Monster in the Mists: Are Long-Buried Memories of Child Abuse Reliable?—Three New Books Tackle a Difficult Issue," *The New York Times Book Review,* May 15, 1994; K. S. Pope, "Memory, Abuse, and Science: Questioning Claims about False Memory Syndrome Epidemic," *American Psychologist,* September 1996.

Pope questions whether false memory syndrome is a scientifically validated syndrome and epidemic. He, like other researchers, considers this "syndrome" a non-psychological term originated by a private foundation founded to support accused parents. In an intelligent discussion of the issues, Pope suggests questions to ask to evaluate claims regarding the existence of false memory syndrome, and the implications for clinical standards. See also Jennifer J. Freyd, *Betrayal Trauma: The Logic of Forgetting Childhood Abuse* (Cambridge: Harvard University Press, 1997). Freyd is a University of Oregon psychologist who herself uncovered memories of abuse that were publicly denied by her parents. Her parents went on to help found the False Memory Syndrome Foundation (a group that considers most recovered memories complete fabrications). Freyd discusses how and why memories can be lost and recovered. She acknowledges the existence of fabricated memories but at the same time explains scientifically many possible mechanisms of forgetting by examining the psychological, cognitive-science, and neurological literature. She believes, as I do, that each claim must be dealt with on a case-by-case basis.

4. Ronnie Janoff-Bulman, "Victims of Violence," in Shirley Fisher and James Reason, eds., *Handbook of Life Stress, Cognition, and Health* (New York: Wiley, 1988). Janoff-Bulman theorizes that people who feel despair over a traumatic event need to integrate that event and come to an understanding of it. Often a person who has experienced a traumatic event will pick the simplest explanation, that he brought it on himself, even when that conclusion is invalid and causes him pain. I would add that although that conclusion causes pain, it also relieves the stress attached to the idea that traumatic events are not within our control.

12. *Responsibility and Blame*

1. See Laura Shapiro, Debra Rosenberg, John F. Lauerman, and Robin Sparkman, "Child Abuse, Rush to Judgment," *Newsweek,* April 19, 1993; L. Wright, "Remembering Satan," *The New Yorker,* 3 parts: May 17, 24, 31, 1993.

2. Taking too much responsibility may stem from a traumatized person needing to feel in control of her life, even if that view of herself is bought at the cost of believing she is to blame for her own mistreatment. If Ronnie Janoff-Bulman is correct, a traumatized person may just pick the simplest explanation, that she brought it on herself. Ronnie Janoff-Bulman, "Victims of Violence," in Shirley Fisher and James Reason, eds., *Handbook of Life Stress, Cognition, and Health* (New York: Wiley, 1988).

For an excellent review of the literature, a good perspective on this debate, and a deeper understanding of the role of responsibility, read Bruce Bower, "Sudden Recall: Adult Memories of Child Abuse Spark a Heated Debate," *Science News,* September 18, 1993: 184–186. For a scholarly discussion of the literature that adds knowledge to our understanding of the nature of memory, forgetting, and responsibility, read Jennifer J. Freyd, *Betrayal Trauma: The Logic of Forgetting Childhood Abuse* (Cambridge: Harvard University Press, 1997). Thanks to Andy Rowland, who knew of my interest, for bringing me a copy of Bower's thoughtful and level-headed summary of the current debate. Most of the other articles on this topic are very sensationalized and one-sided, including many reviews of books on the subject in *The New York Times Book Review* and the investigative reporting in *The New Yorker*. (See also n. 3, chap. 10.)

In "Sudden Recall" and "The Survivor Syndrome: Childhood Sexual Abuse Leaves a Controversial Trail of Aftereffects" (*Science News*, September 25, 1993: 202–204), Bower discusses the views of the main debaters on the subject. Bower reviews the ideas of Judith Herman, a psychiatrist from Harvard Medical School, who thinks that false complaints are rare and that most survivors of actual abuse blame themselves:

> the new emphasis on adult memories of early sexual abuse . . . [is] a healthy antidote to decades of legal and psychiatric neglect suffered by abused individuals. Until recently . . . perpetrators of child sexual abuse committed virtually "perfect crimes": Their young victims rarely reported the offense to other family members or police, the criminal justice system treated the few accusations that arose with suspicion, and clinicians assumed that incest and sexual abuse hardly ever occurred. As a result, most disclosures of childhood sexual abuse have come from adults, who report either having kept the information secret on purpose or recovering memories of abuse after a period of amnesia. . . . To further complicate matters, psychological trauma creates a conflict between the wish to deny horrible events one has experienced and the wish to speak out about them. . . . Thus, people who survive atrocities often piece their stories together in contradictory and fragmented ways as they try both to expose and to expunge their past.

Herman and many therapists believe in some form of delayed recall, what others call "repressed" or "dissociated" memories. Critics of this view—the most prominent being Elizabeth Loftus, a psychologist at the University of Washington—think that we cannot distinguish true repressed memories from false ones because we do not have the tools. Loftus believes repressed or delayed memories are uncommon. For further understanding of the subject of false memory, read Loftus's classic study, "The Reality of Repressed Memories," *American Psychologist*, May 1993: 518–537. David Holmes, a psychologist at the University of Kansas, who is on the board of the False Memory Syndrome Foundation, goes one step further and argues that there is no such thing as repression. This view has brought its own backlash, with many prominent scientists contending that no data support the existence of a "false memory syndrome." Andrew Levin, a psychiatrist at Holliswood Hospital in New York City, finds that survivors who explore their history of abuse often improve. This fits with what I have found: Often the most destructive aspect of abuse is the damage to trust and the effects of having kept the abuse secret from others and/or oneself. Bower quotes Lucy Berliner, a social worker at a sexual assault center in Seattle: "Symptom checklists cannot establish that someone was sexually abused. But I'm not persuaded that therapists commonly diagnose sexual abuse with checklists or engage in a wholesale tendency to talk people into recalling childhood abuse."

Bower summarizes the thinking of the main theoreticians and practitioners in the field (with the exception of Freyd and Schacter, whose theories of the nature of memory and forgetting of traumatic material were not yet published). Bower reports that John Krystal at Yale University School of Medicine discovered that stress actually interferes with glutamate and the related neurotransmitter aspartate, which Krystal theorizes may contribute to post-traumatic stress disorder and other dissociative disorders. According to Krystal, it is not yet clear whether the biological response to stress prevents memories from forming in the first place or blocks the retrieval of memories later. But this discovery speaks to those who have questioned the existence of dissociation, such as Fred Frankel of Beth Israel and Harvard, who is on the advisory board of the False Memory Syndrome Foundation. (See Fred Frankel, "Discovering New Memories in Psychotherapy—Childhood Revisited, Fantasy, or Both?" *New England Journal of Medicine*, August 31, 1995.

Extremist, emotionally based assumptions made on either side of the issue do a great deal of harm. There are those who believe that if you have an eating disorder or a diagnosis of borderline personality or even if you merely claim victimization, you must have been abused. There are those who believe that if you don't remember being abused as a child until the memory is uncovered later, such as in the course of therapy, you must be experiencing a false memory, be naively influenced by your therapist, or be lying. However, if it generates further, much-needed research into this area, the debate can deepen our knowledge and understanding of the causes, effects, and cures of abuse, as well as the nature of memory.

ABOUT THE AUTHOR

Terry Vance, Ph.D., has been a psychotherapist for twenty-eight years. She studied at Carleton College and the University of California at Berkeley and did her doctoral training in clinical psychology at Duke University. She is the mother of two sons and lives with her husband of thirty-one years in Chapel Hill, North Carolina. She is director of Psychology Associates, where she specializes in group and family therapy. Her work also includes individual therapy and supervision of graduate students and mental health professionals.